Secret
INGREDIENTS

Step-by-step "recipes" for creating meaningful gifts

NANCY O'DELL

Secret
INGREDIENTS

Creative Memories
3001 Clearwater Road
St. Cloud, MN 56301
(800) 468-9335
www.creativememories.com

ISBN 9780615541990

Special thanks to design team members:
Jill Klasen
Lisa Dickinson
Ginger Williams
Cindy Liebel
Christa Paustenbaugh
Jen Lessinger
Melissa Ullmann

Photography by Ulrica Wihlborg Photography (www.ulricawihlborg.com), pages 9, 12, 16-18, 20, 32-34, 36, 91, 143, 144, 184, covers.

TABLE OF CONTENTS

This book is dedicated to my sweet mom and dad for expressing their love in so many ways and for documenting it in scrapbook albums for us to remember for years to come. And also to my husband, Keith, and our children, Ashby, Carson, and Tyler, for their support and love and for making the most wonderful memories with me each and every day! And to the entire Creative Memories team . . . everything you cook up is sweet!

PROLOGUE

Earlier this year I saw a Facebook post from Tom Hanks, the wonderful actor. It was Tom's birthday and he had uploaded a photo of the plaque he'd received from his grandchild. In the middle of the plaque were tiny, painted imprints of his grandchild's feet.

It was adorable. And I remember Tom's proud post: "Perfect birthday gift, no?"

Now think about that for a minute. Is it surprising? When we were young, the perfect gift was usually the biggest or the flashiest or the noisiest. Later, the perfect gift became the one that made us look better or go faster or go farther. Somewhere in there, money crept in and the perfect gift became the one with the highest price tag.

But sooner or later we all come around and understand that the **best** gifts are the ones that connect us. They're the gifts that remind us of the people we love most and that help us remember the moments that really matter.

And my favorite thing about giving gifts from the heart is that there's as much joy in giving as there is in receiving. There's a sense of satisfaction that comes in creating something unique and special. It's a feeling you'll never find in a department store.

In my years in Hollywood I've seen some incredible gifts. I've seen big. I've seen showy. I've seen expensive. And I've seen some that would make you scratch your head. But the gifts that stick – the ones that really deliver a message of love – are the ones that have some heart put into them. Those are the ones that stand the test of time. So, for my part, I'll always take the love in the albums my mom gave me over the trendy trinket or gadget of the week.

INTRODUCTION

I find it a little bit ironic that so many of us will spend hours and hours trudging from store to store, surfing online and wracking our brains to come up with just the right gift idea. But if I suggest creating a gift from the heart, I'll hear, "Oh, I just don't have time." Really?

As much as I love my scrapbooks (and anyone who knows me or has read my book, "Full of Love," knows how much I love my scrapbook albums), a gift doesn't have to be a monster photo album in order to show and share love. Some of the gift ideas you'll find in this book are much simpler. They're delightfully special little ways to let the people you love know how special they are to you. Bottom line, they can be easy to do.

So what's it going to take to make it happen? Some photos, for starters. Depending on the project, you might ask family members for help gathering family photos. Sometimes it helps to talk with family and friends and get different perspectives on events and moments you remember. Mostly though, you just need love and a desire to share it.

Here are a few other things to keep in mind as you begin to look through this book and get started:

1. Use these ideas as great jumping off points ... then customize them. For example, maybe we made the project for Grandma, but you know your sister would love something like this. Go for it!

2. Whenever we show computer-printed journaling in this book, please feel free to use your own handwritten words.

3. Some of these projects just show you a few pages to get started. We had too many ideas to share to include full albums for every project! So repeat the pages you like best, or do your own thing. If it's from the heart, it will be perfect.

4. Every cookbook tells you exactly what to use and how to create the recipe. So does this one! But, as any chef knows, you can always customize the recipe to suit your tastes. This book is just like that – let our recipes inspire you!

5. Unless otherwise noted, Creative Memories Tape Runner was used on each project as the adhesive of choice.

One last thing: For the recipes you'll find here, I call for ingredients you can get from a Creative Memories Consultant* because I really believe in the amazing quality and durability of Creative Memories products. I love the passion and commitment of the people I've worked with there – both the home-based Consultants and the folks in the corporate office.

That being said, the really important message in this book is that the people you love need to know how you feel. And you have the power to brighten their lives and lift their spirits in quick, fun, beautiful ways. Use the ideas in this book to do that. No matter what products you choose, I promise it will be among the best gifts that person has ever received. Now, go for it!

*If you don't have a Creative Memories Consultant, you can find one at www.creativememories.com (.ca).

Everyday Gifts

Everybody loves you on your birthday. There's a card waiting for you at the office, and everyone's signed it. There's a cake waiting for you at home, with candles and everything. Your Facebook wall is all lit up with wishes for a "HAPPY B-DAY!! :)" from people you barely remember friending.

Special love comes in between birthdays. It comes every day. These are gifts for a family member, for a friend, for a precious child, for a host whose hospitality you enjoyed or for a co-worker who could use a little pick-me-up. These are ideas to celebrate and say the little things for which we don't often find the time. Those are the things that mean the most.

Everyone celebrates the milestones in life. But it's the quiet (or loud) spaces in between those milestones that form who we are and speak to what we love most.

Chapter 1 Recipes

Chapter 1 Recipes

page 18

What is an "I hope" project?

I believe that every parent has all sorts of hopes and dreams for their children. But how will our kids know what those hopes and dreams are if we don't tell them? Child psychologist Dr. Ken Condrell (who I interviewed in "Full of Love") says that creating albums is "a parent's secret weapon for raising happy, healthy and confident kids." It's so easy. Create an "I hope" project for your kids. For your grandkids. For your spouse or best friend. Let them know what you hope for them and see the difference it makes. If you'd like to learn more about this movement, please visit the Hope in Action website at www.hopeinaction.com.

page 38

page 44

THINGS WE LOVE

Album pages for an 8 x 8 scrapbook album

The things we *Love* to do *together* as a family.

Page 1

Ingredients:

8 x 8 Coverset

8 x 8 White Scrapbook Pages

Yellow Cardstock

Cloud Cardstock

Pink Lemonade Cardstock

Royal Blue Cardstock

White Shimmer Cardstock

12-inch Rotary Trimmer

Personal Trimmer

Tape Runner

Sometimes the best gift you can give every member of your family (and yourself) is a simple reminder of how good life is. Keith and I wake up each morning knowing how blessed and lucky we are. It's something of which we never want to lose sight. And, just as important, as the kids grow and head off to college or out to start families of their own, we want them to always remember the good times that have brought us together as a family. So this quick, simple little 8 x 8 album, with no frills or embellishments, is an ongoing tribute to the things we all love to do together as a family. And we love it!

Instructions:

Page 1:
- Run a piece of Cloud Cardstock through your printer or handwrite a title for the scrapbook.
- Cut Cloud Cardstock to measure $6\frac{1}{2}''$ x $5\frac{1}{4}''$ and adhere it to the page.

Page 2:
- Print one picture to measure 7" x 5." Adhere to page.
- Print or handwrite journaling on Cloud Cardstock to measure $7\frac{1}{2}''$ x $1\frac{1}{2}.''$

Page 3:
- Print 9 photos to measure 2" x 2." Arrange them on the page in a grid as shown.

Page 4:
- Print 4 photos to measure 2" x 3" and adhere them along the bottom of the page.
- Print a photo to measure 4" x 4." Adhere it in the upper-left corner of the page, as shown.
- Print or handwrite journaling on Pink Lemonade Cardstock to measure 3" x 3."

Page 5:
- Print 3 photos to measure $2\frac{1}{2}''$ x 6" and adhere them to page, as shown.

Page 6:
- Print 8 photos to measure 2" x 3". Adhere to upper and lower edges of page as shown.
- Print or handwrite journaling on White Shimmer Cardstock to measure $7\frac{1}{4}''$ x $1\frac{1}{4}.''$ Mat that on Royal Blue Cardstock to measure $7\frac{1}{2}''$ x $1\frac{1}{2}.''$ Adhere to page.

Page 7:
- Print photo to measure 8" x 8." Adhere to page.

Page 8:
- Print 4 photos to measure 3" x 3." Adhere to layout in a grid as shown.
- Print or handwrite journaling on Yellow Cardstock to measure $5\frac{3}{4}''$ x $1\frac{1}{4}.''$ Adhere to page.

Page 9:
- Print 4 photos to measure 3" x 3." Arrange them in a grid on the page as shown.

Continued

Family Game Night...

We love an evening with the kids playing their favorite board games. It's an evening filled with laughter and a little competition.

Page 2

Page 3

Storytime...

Reading to the kids has always been a wonderful way to connect one on one. Having them share what their little minds are thinking about is definitely worth hearing.

Page 4

Page 5

Cooking & Baking...

Whether we are baking, cooking or decorating...we have fun.
We love filling our tummies with things we've made together. Nothing beats a
little love from our oven covered in sweetness and sprinkles!

Page 6

Page 7

Traveling...

As a family, we love vacationing in our favorite
destinations. We are very grateful for the opportunities
we have been given to spend time away together.

Page 8

Page 9

"I HOPE" POSTER

Digital layout for a 16 x 24 poster

Our sweet & playful Ashby,

Life is *beautiful*

We hope...

...you will do for others and understand that you can make a difference

...you love and enjoy learning

...you will always know how to laugh and spend a lot of time doing just that

...you will have a special bond with your brothers

...you will always remember how special you were to your Grandma Betty and are to Da, Grandpa & Grandma.

...you will know and feel you can count on your mom and dad to be there for you ALWAYS!

...you never forget how VERY much we love you!!!

Love, Mama & Poppy

As a parent, you can give your kids love. You can offer them advice. You can share your hopes and dreams. But whether those things will actually sink in is anybody's guess. Improve your odds by keeping the important things right in front of their faces. (And improve the odds they'll pay attention by including their pictures!) **That's** *what makes a personalized, custom poster more valuable than one of a cat in sunglasses. Consider making one for your child at any age (graduation, wedding…) Maybe make one for a spouse, for a parent or for a dear friend who's moving along.*

Ingredients:

StoryBook Creator 4.0 Software

Gratitude Series Digital Kit

Font: Adler

Font: Dear Sarah Rg

Instructions:

- Create a new Wall Print project and choose 16″ x 24″ Portrait. Add Gratitude Paper 12 to the bottom of your layout.
- Add a 16″ x 13″ photo across center area. Add a heavy shadow.
- Add Gratitude Paper 06 to the top. Apply a paper tear to the bottom of the paper. Add a heavy shadow.
- Add the green ribbon and cream ribbon to the top. Add a heavy shadow and a Half Ellipse edge to the cream ribbon, as shown.

- Add the Orange Square Tag. Add title as desired. Add the "Life is beautiful" tag.
- Add the green bar, title and journaling, as shown.
- Add the "Find the joy" title. Under the Cut & Fill tab, create a rectangle and select the letters of the title. Delete, leaving only the swirls. Under the Cut & Fill tab, change the color to white. Under the Format tab, change the opacity to 20 percent. Copy and paste twice. Size and align as shown.

THANKFUL FOR YOU

12 x 12 Album Page for a Page Frame

Sometimes it's the simple things that speak volumes without saying a word. There's nothing deep or introspective about this Page Frame, but I love it. It's just a single 12 x 12 album page placed in a Page Frame. But it reminds me of some of the most precious blessings in my life, and that's important. Think about a simple gift like this for grandparents, for distant relatives ... or for your own family.

Ingredients:

Gratitude Paper & Photo Mat Pack

Gratitude Embellishment Pack

Espresso Cardstock

Brown Dual-Tip Pen

Tearing Tool

Tape Runner

Foam Squares

Instructions:

• Use a sheet of Espresso Cardstock as the base for your page.

• Print photo to measure 8" x 12." Adhere to the right side of the page.

• Using the Tearing Tool, tear a sheet of the brown patterned paper to 4½" x 12." Adhere to the left side of the layout, overlapping photo.

• Cut 2 pieces of paper ribbon (blue and cream) to measure 12 inches. Adhere both at the top of the page.

• Print 2 photos to measure 2½" x 2½." Adhere to blue photo mats cut to 2¾" x 2¾." Adhere to page using Foam Squares.

• Add title sticker to blue die-cut tag. Adhere to page.

• Using the Brown Dual-Tip Pen, journal on green die-cut tag. Adhere to page.

• Add a round green epoxy sticker to page, as shown.

GRATITUDE ALBUM

Album pages for a 12 x 12 scrapbook album

find joy

The things you do that
make us smile...

Page 1

My mother and father taught me to always say please and thank you. But there are times when "thank you" just isn't nearly enough. So a while back we decided that my dad needed a special album to let him know how grateful we all were. There was no birthday, no occasion – just years of built-up love and gratitude. Everyone in the family sent pictures and shared what they were grateful to Dad for and expressed how much they appreciate him. Then I was able to type all those up and lay them out into an amazing book that shows Dad just why and how much he's loved. This was really an easy gift to create, since everyone helped – basically doing their own page.

Ingredients:

12 x 12 Gratitude Coverset

12 x 12 White Scrapbook Pages

Gratitude Paper & Photo Mat Pack

Gratitude Title Stickers

Gratitude Embellishment Pack

Gratitude Scallop Tearing Tool

12-inch Rotary Trimmer

Foam Squares

Tape Runner

Font: American Typewriter

Instructions:

Page 1

• Use the brown decorative paper as the base for your layout.

• Adhere a blue photo mat and a 4″ x 6″ photo.

• Adhere an 8-inch piece of blue paper ribbon, as shown, tearing one end.

• Place the blue die-cut embellishment on the ribbon with Foam Squares. Add journaling as desired.

• Using Foam Squares, adhere the brown circle die cut. Add the "Find the Joy" title sticker.

Continued

Page 2

- Use the light-blue diamond-patterned paper as the base of your layout.
- Cut a piece of brown checkered paper, following the foil pattern. Trim to $3\frac{1}{2}''$ wide and adhere to the right edge of the page.
- Adhere 2 brown/green circle die-cut embellishments as shown.
- Mat two 4" x 6" photos on cream mats and adhere. Add a 2" x 3" photo.
- Place a title sticker in the bottom-left corner.
- Add journaling to a $2\frac{1}{4}''$ x 3" white photo mat.

Page 3

- Use the brown floral-patterned paper as the base of your layout.
- Adhere a 3" x 12" piece of blue diamond-patterned paper $1\frac{3}{4}$ inches from the right edge.
- Use the remainder of the brown checkered paper you cut for page 2, and adhere it to the left edge.
- Adhere a brown die-cut embellishment.
- Mat a 4" x 6" photo on a blue photo mat and place in lower center of page. Add an additional 4" x 6" photo. Adhere a 2" x 3" photo to a $2\frac{1}{2}''$ x $3\frac{1}{2}''$ piece of green photo mat. Adhere to layout.

Page 4

- Use the cream floral-patterned paper as the base of your layout.
- Use the Scallop Tearing Tool to tear a piece of brown paper to 2 inches wide, using the tool's larger scallop. Place it so that the straight edge is 3½ inches from the bottom of the page.
- Adhere 2 orange photo mats vertically as shown. Place a brown photo mat horizontally on top. Adhere a 4" x 6" photo. Adhere the "One is rich..." title sticker in the bottom corner of the right photo mat.
- Use Foam Squares to adhere a brown die-cut embellishment and place a brown/green epoxy sticker in the center.

Page 5

- Use the orange circle-patterned paper as the base of your layout.
- Cut cream paper to 8" x 10½" and position as shown.
- Adhere 2 brown photo mats with 4" x 6" photos.
- Cut a piece of cream paper ribbon to 9½ inches, trimming the ends as shown. Using a Foam Square, adhere a cream epoxy sticker on top.
- Add journaling as desired on cream photo mats.

Continued

Page 6

- Use the blue diamond-patterned paper as the base of your layout. Cut a piece of green circle-patterned paper to 3″ x 12″ and add it along the left edge. Cut a piece of cream/blue circle-patterned paper to 7″ x 9″ and add it as shown.
- Cut a 9-inch piece of cream paper ribbon. Adhere above the cream/blue circle-patterned paper.
- Adhere a blue and a green photo mat, each with a 4″ x 6″ photo. Add a 3″ x 4″ photo.
- Use Foam Squares to adhere a blue die-cut embellishment and place the title sticker on top.

Page 7

- Use the blue diamond-patterned paper as the base of your layout. Cut a piece of green circle-patterned paper to 3″ x 12″ and place it along the right edge.
- Cut a piece of cream/blue circle-patterned paper to 7″ x 9″ and add it, as shown. (Make sure it aligns with the smaller rectangle on page 6.)
- Cut a 9-inch piece of cream paper ribbon. Adhere above the cream/blue circle-patterned paper.
- Adhere a green photo mat with a 4″ x 6″ photo. Add two 2″ x 3″ photos.
- Adhere a blue die-cut embellishment under the cream/blue circle-patterned paper.
- Journal as desired on a 3¼″ x 2″ piece of cream photo mat.

Page 8

- Use the blue diamond-patterned paper as the base of your layout. Using the Gratitude Scallop Tearing Tool, cut a cream/gold-foil paper to $5\frac{1}{2}''$ wide using the smaller scallop tear. Adhere to the right edge of the layout.
- Cut a light-green photo mat to $4\frac{1}{2}''$ x 5" and add a 4" x $4\frac{1}{2}''$ photo. Place it in the upper-left corner.
- Adhere a $3\frac{1}{2}''$ x 4" photo in the upper-right corner.
- Adhere a green photo mat tucked under the scalloped side of the cream/gold-foil paper. Add two $\frac{3}{4}''$ x 4" photos.
- Adhere a $4\frac{1}{2}''$ x 5" green photo mat as shown. Add a 4" x 4" photo.
- Add title sticker.

Page 9

- Use the green circle-patterned paper as the base of your layout.
- Use the Scallop Tearing Tool to tear a cream/gold-foil paper to $5\frac{1}{2}$ inches wide using the smaller scallop side and attach it to the left edge of the layout.
- Cut a green photo mat to $1\frac{1}{2}$ inches wide. Position so it aligns with the green photo mat from the previous page. Adhere the rectangle epoxy sticker.
- Adhere a 4" x 4" photo to a $4\frac{1}{2}''$ x $4\frac{1}{2}''$ blue photo mat and add to upper-left corner.
- Adhere a blue photo mat with a 4" x 6" photo in the lower-right.
- Cut a cream photo mat to $4\frac{5}{8}''$ x $4\frac{1}{2}$." Using the Scallop Tearing Tool, tear the right edge using the smaller scallop side. Adhere to the layout. Add journaling as desired.

Continued

Page 10

- Use the green diamond-patterned paper as the base of your layout. Using the Gratitude Scallop Tearing Tool, tear brown floral-patterned paper to $5\frac{1}{2}''$ wide using the larger scallop side. Adhere to the top edge of the layout.
- Adhere a 12-inch piece of green paper ribbon.
- Add two 4" x 6" photos, as shown.
- Cut a green die-cut embellishment to $3\frac{1}{2}$ inches. Adhere to the left edge of the layout.
- Using Foam Squares, adhere a green die-cut embellishment (backwards, so the white side is showing). Apply a brown epoxy sticker in the center.
- Cut a white photo mat to $3\frac{1}{4}''$ x 3," add journaling as desired and place, as shown.

Page 11

- Use the green diamond-patterned paper as the base of your layout. Using the Gratitude Scallop Tearing Tool, tear brown floral-patterned paper to $5\frac{1}{2}$ inches wide using the larger scallop side. Adhere to the top edge of the layout.
- Adhere a $10\frac{1}{2}$-inch piece of green paper ribbon, with the end torn as shown. Add the "Blessings" title sticker. Using Foam Squares, place a green die-cut embellishment (backward, so the white side is showing) on the ribbon and add a brown epoxy sticker in the center.
- Add two 4" x 6" photos.
- Cut a green die-cut embellishment to $3\frac{1}{2}$ inches. Adhere to the right edge of the layout.
- Trim a cream photo mat to fit the space as shown and add journaling as desired.

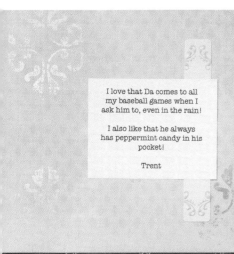

I love that Da comes to all
my baseball games when I
ask him to, even in the rain!

I also like that he always
has peppermint candy in his
pocket!

Trent

Page 12

- Use brown patterned paper as the base of your layout. Cut 2 pieces of orange circle-patterned paper to 6" x 6." Adhere each as shown to the layout.
- Cut 2 green photo mats to 4½-inch squares and adhere. Add a 4-inch square photo to each.
- Adhere an orange title die cut vertically in the upper left. Trim a cream circle-patterned photo mat and add journaling as desired.
- Adhere a green circle die cut. Add the "Blessed" circle title sticker over the top of the die cut and finish with an orange epoxy sticker in the center.

Page 13

- Use brown checkered paper as the base of your layout. Cut 2 pieces of orange circle-patterned paper to 6" x 6." Adhere each, as shown.
- Cut 2 green photo mats to 4½-inch squares and adhere. Add a 4-inch square photo to one and two 2" x 3" photos to the other.
- Adhere the title sticker along with green/orange epoxy stickers.
- Cut a green die-cut title to 3½ inches. Adhere it vertically as shown. Add a 6-inch cream paper ribbon and top off with a green epoxy sticker.
- Adhere a 2" x 3" photo.

Gotta get it write

Today it's so easy to print out your journaling in some insanely beautiful font. There's no doubt it looks great. You can spell check it. You can play with it until everything's ... perfect. And that's what concerns me. Personally, I prefer the intimate look of handwritten journaling. Just seeing someone's handwriting can bring up so many memories of that person. The album shown at right that our family collectively made for Papa Z (Keith's father) is a perfect example. I love the handwritten notes from Papa Z's children and grandchildren. The effort Ashby put into writing just her name ... it's all so sweet and adds that special touch of realness to the gifts you are making. So it's a personal choice. But every now and then, I really encourage you to try handwriting.

WHAT I LEARNED FROM SPORTS

Album pages for an 11 x 14 Expandable PicFolio® Album

find the joy in life

There's no crying in baseball, but there will be crying in the game of life.

It's okay though, because there will also be laughing, loving and so much fun.

And through it all, we'll be cheering for you! Love always, Mama & Poppy

Both Keith and I grew up with a passion for sports. (We both wore #4 for our high school basketball teams!) Being part of a team... Giving your absolute best... Greeting victory with class and defeat with grace... These are lessons we want to pass on to the boys and Ashby as they find the activities that inspire them. Your kids will play games, even if it's just hitting a tee ball in preschool. Try making an ongoing album of this, adding new photos and new lessons as your kids grow. A PicFolio® Album makes this so simple, since all you do is slide in the photos, decorations and journaling.

Ingredients:

11 x 14 Expandable PicFolio® Album

Gratitude Photo Album Accents

Instructions:

- Place fillers, photos and journaling cards in desired spaces.
- Add title stickers to fillers as desired.
- Journal on fillers as desired.

GRANDPARENT MUG

Personalized Coffee Mugs

A good, hot cup of coffee could change the way you look at your morning. But a good, hot cup of coffee in a beautifully designed mug featuring the faces of your grandkids? That's a guaranteed good day. I love the way these full-coverage designs let you go beyond "#1 Grandpa" on a white background. Create a perfect, practical gift for your parents that will get used over and over!

Ingredients

StoryBook Creator 4.0 Software

Gratitude Series Digital Kit

Font: Adler

Font: Satisfaction

Instructions:

Grandpa coffee mug

- Open a custom 8½" x 4.47" layout. Add Gratitude Paper 04 to your project.
- Add 3" x 4½" photo. Mat your photo with Gratitude Paper 10 paper.
- Add two of the Green Flourish Embellishments. Under the Color Tab, convert to Sepia. Rotate and align as shown.
- Add the Blue Ribbon. Under the Format tab, add a heavy shadow.
- Add the Blue Horizontal Tag. Under the Format tab, add a heavy shadow.
- Add the word "Grandpa" in the font Adler to the tag.

Grandma coffee mug

- Open a custom 8½" x 4.47" layout. Add Gratitude Paper 07 to your project.
- Add Gratitude Paper 06 and Gratitude Paper 04. Align to the top and bottom as shown. Under the Cut & Fill tab, select Straight – Shaped Edge – Half Ellipse. Align along the top and bottom of your papers. Erase the unwanted shaded area to create the edge as shown. Under the Format tab, add a heavy shadow to each.
- Add a 4¾" x 4.6" photo. Under the Format Photos tab, change your mat width to 1 and sample to color from the ivory in the paper.
- Add the Blue Word embellishment across the top.
- Add the Orange Flower and Blue Circle Epoxy embellishments.
- Add the Blessings Banner. Add the text "Grandma's." Change the color to match the ivory in the paper. Add the "Find the Joy" title. Under the Cut & Fill tab, change your title to ivory. Cut off the title leaving only the flourish. Size and align as if it's coming off the "G" in Grandma.
- Copy and paste the title. Change to orange. Align, slightly shifted behind the ivory title. Add a light shadow to each under the Format tab.
- Upload project to digital.creativememories.com to place your order.

JUST US

Design for a 12 x 12 custom album cover

We can only be said to
be alive in those moments
when our **hearts** are
conscious of our treasures.
-Thornton Wilder

LOVE

Making an album for someone can make them feel special and loved. Put someone's picture on the cover of the album, and your gift goes to a whole new level. This is a fantastic gift for new parents, graduates or brides and grooms. Or just imagine the cover you could make for an album commemorating that special trip! In my case, it's a great way to house all the special photos of a mom and her sweet daughter.

Ingredients:

StoryBook Creator 4.0 Software – Advanced Mode
Gratitude Series Digital Kit

Instructions:

- Create a new You Create It Album – 12 x 12. Add Gratitude Paper 09 to the background.
- Add Gratitude Paper 16. Under the Cut & Fill Tab, cut the paper into a rectangle. Size and align as shown.
- Add Gratitude Paper 07. Under the Cut & Fill Tab, select Straight – Paper Rip. Rip the edge of each side of the paper. Size and align as shown.
- Add a $4^3/_4''$ x $7^1/_2''$ photo. Under the Format Tab, add a heavy shadow.
- Add the Blue Word Border embellishment across the bottom of the layout. Add the "Love" embellishment.

- Add the Pin embellishment. Under the Cut & Fill tab, use the magic wand to select the brown head of the pin. Copy the selected area. Under the Color Tab, select Adjust Hue. Use the eyedropper to sample the blue color from the Blue Word Border. Adjust the saturation to match as well as possible.
- Add the "We can only be..." title. Under the Cut & Fill tab, change the color to brown to match your layout.
- Upload project to digital.creativememories.com to place your order.

I HOPE YOU KNOW, MOM

12 x 12 Page for a Magnetic Everyday Display

This is another idea that uses a Magnetic Everyday Display as both a gift and a message board. Do you have some important thoughts to share with your mom? Put them together beautifully on a display board so Mom can hang them up and see them all the time! And, at the end of it all, Mom's left with a display board she can update and use any way she likes. (Although if my daughter ever gave me a sweet note like this, I'd never change it at all. Ever!)

Ingredients:

Sleek White Everyday Display

Fabulous Tone-on-Tone Paper

Fabulous Designer-Print Paper

Fabulous Paper Buttons

Fabulous Paper Ribbon

White Cardstock

White Swirly ABC/123 Stickers

Scallop Circle Maker

Tag Maker

Blossom Place 'n' Punch

12-inch Rotary Trimmer

Border Maker System (with Scallop Stitch Cartridge)

Custom Cutting System (with Jumbo Circle Pattern)

Foam Squares

Tape Runner

Instructions:

• Use a piece of pink paper as a base for the layout.

• Cut out a teal circle using the inside of the Jumbo Circle and the green blade.

• Add it to the layout, as shown.

• Add a 12″ x 4″ strip of gray patterned paper to the bottom of the layout.

• Using the Border Maker, cut a 12-inch border of pink striped paper and adhere it along the top of your gray rectangle.

• Add a 12-inch strip of both teal and white paper ribbon across the layout, as shown.

• Use the Tag Maker to punch 2 paper tags from orange paper and add to the top-left and middle-right.

• Mat 4″ x 4″ and 6″ x 4″ photos on White Cardstock and add to the layout.

• Punch several flowers with the Blossom Place 'n' Punch and Scallop Circle Maker. Add paper buttons to the centers with Foam Squares.

• Add the flowers to the layout with Foam Squares.

• Add titles to the photos with ABC Stickers.

• Print or handwrite journaling on White Cardstock and add to the layout, as shown.

LOVE NOTES

4½ x 6½ note cards

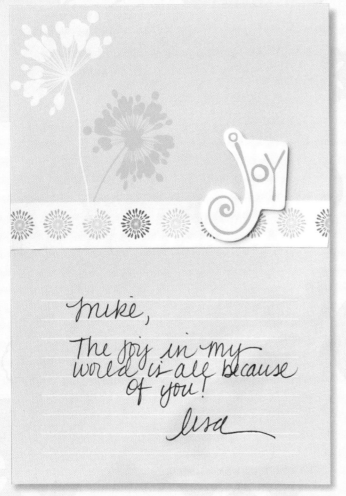

Love Note 1

Love Note 2

Remember when passing notes was so important and exciting? Get back to that with adorable little love notes like these. If you can find an hour, you can knock out a whole stack of handmade cards to keep handy for any day and every day! For some sentiments, you can even write the note in advance so you're ready to give it on a whim. How's **that** *for planned spontaneity?*

Ingredients:

Reflections Designer-Print Paper

Reflections Storybox

Reflections Title Stickers

Reflections Paper Flowers

Reflections Paper Ribbon

White Shimmer Cardstock

Black Dual-Tip Pen

All-Purpose Scissors

Lovable Mini Pocket Punch

Corner Maker

Sweet Heart Maker

Precision Point Adhesive

Foam Squares

Tape Runner

Instructions:

Love Note 1

• Adhere strip of paper ribbon across a light-green journaling mat.

• Apply title sticker with a Foam Square.

Love Note 2

• Adorn a dark-gray journaling mat with white paper flower and green leaves.

• Use striped ribbon to make a loop.

• Adhere ribbon loop to center of flower.

Continued

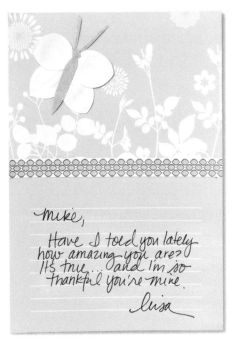

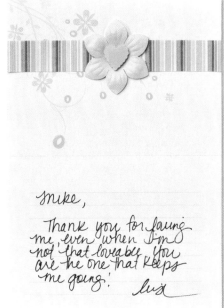

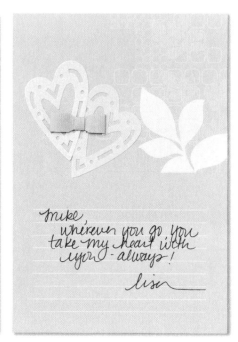

Love Note 3

- Create butterfly by cutting apart white flower petals and using 4 petals as wings.
- Trim gray paper into body shape and adhere your butterfly to a blue journaling mat.
- Adhere the paper ribbon across mat.

Love Note 4

- Adhere strip of striped paper ribbon across mat.
- Adhere blue paper flower in center.
- Use Lovable Mini Pocket Punch to punch a heart from green paper.
- Adhere heart to center of flower using Foam Squares.

Love Note 5

- Use Sweet Heart Maker to punch hearts from White Shimmer Cardstock.
- Adhere to a light-gray journaling card using the Precision Point Adhesive.
- Create a small bow using green paper ribbon and adhere it on top of the hearts.

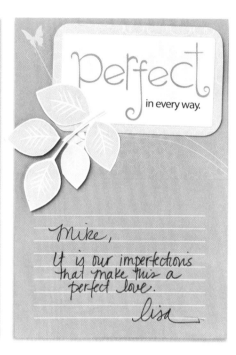

Love Note 6

- Adhere paper flowers across the top of a green journaling mat.

Love Note 7

- Apply title stickers to green striped paper and use your Corner Maker to round the outside corners.
- Adhere it to a blue journaling mat with Foam Squares.

Love Note 8

- Apply title stickers to blue paper and use Corner Maker to round outside corners. Adhere to blue journaling mat with Foam Squares.
- Use scissors to trim leaves with stem from Reflections Designer-Print Paper. Adhere over title.

"I HOPE" DISPLAY

12 x 12 page for a Magnetic Everyday Display

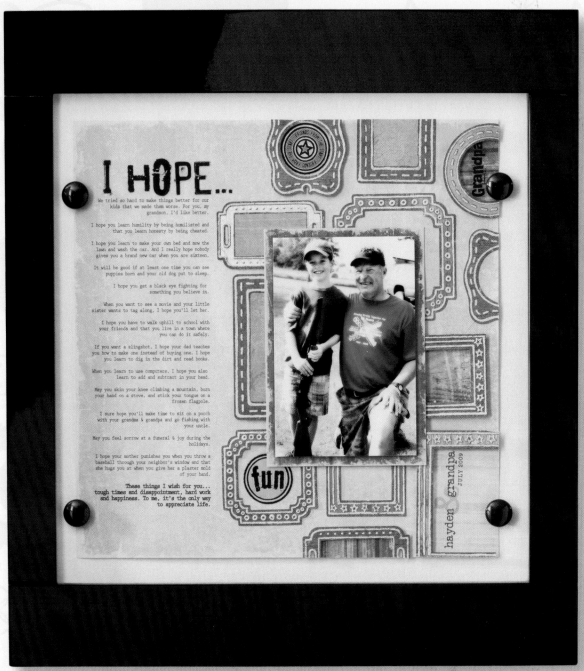

By the time you get to be a grandparent, you've learned a thing or two. (And one of the things you've probably learned is that no one captured the wisdom of a generation quite like Paul Harvey!) In this project, we've taken the Paul Harvey broadcast excerpt that Grandpa chose, added a photo and created a memorable message. While this page would work wonderfully in a scrapbook album, we've put it on a Magnetic Everyday Display to hang on the wall and always remind Hayden of Grandpa's advice. This project also works great for Grandma to create with her words of wisdom!

Ingredients:

Sleek Black Magnetic Everyday Display

Rugged Tone-on-Tone Paper

Rugged Designer-Print Paper

Rugged Storybox Photo Mats

Rugged Title Stickers

Rugged Decorative ABC Stickers

Rugged Paper Tags

Rugged Paper Frames

Personal Trimmer

12-inch Rotary Trimmer

Foam Squares

Tape Runner

Instructions:

- Print or handwrite journaling down left side of blue patterned paper.
- Arrange tags and paper frames on right side of page, layering some with patterned paper and stickers. Adhere to page, using Foam Squares on a few tags. Trim tags that hang over the paper edge with a Rotary Trimmer.
- Apply ABC stickers for title. Mat photo on blue photo mat. Adhere over tags on right side of page.

Paul Harvey Broadcast Excerpt
(written by Lee Pitts)

We tried so hard to make things better for our kids that we made them worse. For my grandchildren, I'd like better.

I hope you learn humility by being humiliated, and that you learn honesty by being cheated. And I really hope nobody gives you a brand new car when you are sixteen.

It will be good if at least one time you can see puppies born and your old dog put to sleep.

I hope you get a black eye fighting for something you believe in.

When you want to see a movie and your little brother wants to tag along, I hope you'll let him.

When you learn to use computers, I hope you also learn to add and subtract in your head.

I sure hope you make time to sit on a porch with your Grandpa and go fishing with your Uncle.

May you feel sorrow at a funeral and joy during the holidays.

These things I wish for you - tough times and disappointment, hard work and happiness. To me, it's the only way to appreciate life.

FAMILY VALUES

Album pages for a 12 x 12 scrapbook album

Joan & Fred Little

circa 1946

Living of LOVE

For just one chance to find
Love was someone that you loved to find
For just the sense to try
To walk ahead and leave the pain behind
If the days aren't easy & the nights are rough
When they ask you what you're thinking of...
Say love, say for me love
Say love, say for me love

Your heart says, "Not again...
what kind of mess have you got me in?"
But when the feeling's there
It can lift you up and take you anywhere
The gravel beneath you & the limbs above
If anybody asks you where you're coming from
Say love, say for me love
Say love, say for me love

Yes, we have uncertainty
and disappointments have to be
and everyday we might be facing more...
Yes, we live in desperate times
with fading words and shaking rhymes
There's only one thing here worth hoping for.
With Lucifer beneath you & God above -
if either one asks you what you're living of
Say love, say for me love

*As a fourth-generation scrapbooker, I've learned firsthand the wonderful things albums can do. One of the most important of those things is capturing the essence of your family's history. With some photos and the stories behind them, you can show your children not only who their great-grandparents were, but what they went through and what lessons they have to share. Now **that's** a gift. We've created this album in paper. Or, using StoryBook Creator 4.0 Software, you could do it digitally and print a copy for everyone in the family.*

Ingredients:

12 x 12 Coverset

12 x 12 Scrapbook Pages

Gratitude Paper & Photo Mat Pack

Gratitude Embellishment Pack

Reflections Title Stickers

Espresso Cardstock

White Cardstock

White Shimmer Cardstock

Brown Sophisticate ABC/123 Stickers

White Simple Monogram Stickers

Brown Dual-Tip Pen

Precious Element Copper Pen

Precious Element Silver Pen

Doodling Templates

All-Purpose Scissors

Lovable Mini Pocket Punches

Scallop Circle Maker

Sweet Heart Maker

Gratitude Scallop Tearing Tool

12-inch Rotary Trimmer (with Straight and Postage Stamp Blades)

Border Maker System (with Picket Fence and Scallop Stitch Cartridges)

Custom Cutting System (with Jumbo Circle Pattern)

Foam Squares

Tape Runner

Instructions:

Page 1

- Print or handwrite journaling at the bottom of White Shimmer Cardstock.
- Adhere 2 brown photo mats above journaling.
- Trim several half-inch strips of blue and green paper and weave together. Adhere to a piece of White Cardstock. Using scissors, cut out a heart shape and adhere, overlapping the right side of the photo mats.

- Using Doodling Templates, trace doodles onto green patterned paper. Trim using scissors. Adhere on the page to the right of the woven heart.
- Use the Scallop Circle Maker to punch out a blue scalloped circle. Using scissors, trim a printed flower from the patterned paper. Layer the printed flower and scalloped circle and adhere over traced doodles. *Continued*

FAMILY

values

When Roy & Neva Peterson began their lives together, it was foundation built of love. They made their home in the rural town of Burdick, Kansas, working as a postman and homemaker and raising three children Larry, Mark, and Candice. The most important legacy they leave to us are the family values so strongly held throughout their lives - hard work, faith, loyalty... and above all else, LOVE.

Roy, Neva & Larry Peterson
June 5, 1949

Page 2

- Add your title to a paper tag using ABC stickers and adhere to bottom of woven heart.
- Use Sweet Heart Maker to punch 2 hearts from orange paper and 1 from White Cardstock. Layer the inside of the white heart onto the outside of an orange heart and adhere to left side of title tag with Foam Squares. Put the 2 orange "inside" hearts next to the green flourish.
- Trim a piece of White Cardstock to mat your photo. Then place it on top of the brown mats, as shown, using Foam Squares.
- Add "stitching" to page elements with Precious Element Silver Pen and Brown Dual-Tip Pen.

Page 2

- Use the Custom Cutting System (blue blade) along the outside edge of the Jumbo Circle Pattern to cut a circle from Espresso Cardstock.
- Use the green blade to cut circles from White Shimmer Cardstock and patterned paper. Using the 12-inch Rotary Trimmer (Straight Blade), cut about a third off the patterned-paper circle and adhere it on top of the White Shimmer circle. Then adhere the White Shimmer circle to the larger Espresso Circle.
- Use the Border Maker to make a picket fence border using Espresso Cardstock. Thread with paper ribbon. Pull up bow loops and adhere to border with green epoxy sticker, as shown. Adhere the border between White Shimmer Cardstock and paper.

- Create title with monogram stickers and ABC stickers. Outline white monogram stickers with copper pen.
- Mount photo on Espresso Cardstock and use Rotary Trimmer (Postage Stamp Blade) to trim a decorative edge. Adhere to page with Foam Squares.
- Using the Scallop Circle Maker, punch 2 circles from green patterned paper. Adhere to the layout with Foam Squares. Add epoxy stickers in the center.
- Print or handwrite journaling on green-patterned paper and cut into strips. Adhere to page.

Page 3

- Print or handwrite quote on the bottom edge of White Shimmer Cardstock.
- Trim a piece of orange patterned paper to 12" x 7." Adhere across center of page.
- Use the Border Maker System (Scallop Stitch Cartridge) to create two 12-inch scalloped borders with Espresso Cardstock. Adhere to top and bottom edges of orange paper.
- Create title with monogram stickers by applying them to blue patterned paper and trimming to $2^{1/4}"$ x 7." Adhere over green paper. Trim the top and bottom edges using the Scallop Tearing Tool. Adhere to a strip of Espresso Cardstock (trimmed to $3^{1/4}"$ x 7") with Foam Squares. Affix to left side of orange paper.
- Use scissors to cut 3 floral designs from patterned paper. Adhere to page, trimming overhang.

Continued

As a serviceman, father, husband and business man, Opa was always led by his loyal heart. It's one of many honorable qualities he possessed, including patience, dedication, faithfulness & diligence.

But the trait I admire most, and that which I will always associate with his life, is loyalty.

LOYAL

"I am sustained by the tranquility of an upright and loyal heart." -PETER STUYVESANT

Page 3

- Mat photos on White Cardstock and trim using 12-inch Rotary Trimmer (Postage Stamp Blade). Adhere to page using Foam Squares.
- Print or handwrite journaling on White Cardstock. Trim into strips and adhere to page.

Page 4

- Create title with ABC stickers. Add journaling below using Brown Dual-Tip Pen or printing with your computer on White Shimmer Cardstock.
- Trim green paper to 4½" x 12." Adhere to left side of White Shimmer Cardstock.
- Create scalloped border using Espresso Cardstock. Adhere next to green paper. Cover the seam with a strip of blue paper ribbon.
- Adhere photo to center of page using Foam Squares. Add blue and green paper tags to lower-left corner. Using the Scallop Circle Maker, punch a scalloped circle from patterned paper and adorn with an epoxy sticker. Adhere between tags. Put a title sticker on blue tag. Write a short caption on a strip of White Cardstock and adhere to green tag.
- Trim out several circles from green patterned paper. Layer over paper using Foam Squares to add dimension.

Note: Use these four page examples to get this great gift started. Then repeat these designs or use your imagination! The important part is to keep capturing your family's history.

Page 4

WHAT YOU'VE TAUGHT ME

Album pages for a 4 x 6 PicFolio® Album

You have taught me the greatness of life by having a sense of humor and laughing out loud.

Life of the Party

made 4 having Fun

Spread 1

The thing I love about these PicFolio® Photo Albums is how fast they are. A 4 x 6 album like this has 12 pages. That's 24 slip-in sleeves. And that's a perfect number for a quick-but-meaningful "I love you" that can last a lifetime. Maybe have everyone in the family make a page, then fill in the blanks with photos. A quick tribute like this can be adapted to come from a parent to a grown child, a wife to her husband, a child to a grandparent....

Ingredients:

4 x 6 PicFolio® Album

Rugged Designer-Print Paper

Rugged Storybox Photo Mats

Rugged Title Stickers

Rugged Paper Frames

Rugged Paper Ribbons

Rugged Paper Tags

Brown Cardstock

Brown Dual-Tip Pen

All-Purpose Scissors

Lovable Mini Pocket Punch

Circle Maker

Personal Trimmer

12-inch Rotary Trimmer

Custom Cutting System (with Circle Patterns)

Precision Point Adhesive

Foam Squares

Tape Runner

Instructions:

• Trim Brown Cardstock to 12 pieces of 4" x 6" pages. Use these as backgrounds.

Spread 1

• On left side, adhere your choice of designer-print paper to background.

• Adhere 4" x 6" photo to cream photo mat. Trim excess, creating a thin frame around photo and adhere to left page. Adhere title sticker to photo.

• On right page, adhere 4½" x 4" printed paper to bottom of background. Adhere a 4" x 1¾" strip cut from a photo mat at top. Cover seams using starred paper ribbon and wrap around the sides.

• Using small Custom Cutting System Circle Pattern, cut a small circle from a cream photo mat. Adhere behind round paper frame. Affix title sticker and adhere to bottom-right corner of page. Add another title sticker above it.

• Using the scallop Lovable Mini Pocket Punch, embellish both pages with hearts. Affix a few with Foam Squares to add dimension.

Spread 2

• On left side, adhere designer-print paper to background.

• Adhere a 3¾" x 3¾" photo to a 4" x 4" square cut from a cream Storybox and adhere to page. Put one paper tag above right of photo and affix title sticker.

• On right side, adhere 4¼" x 4" printed paper to top of background and 4¼" x 2¼" ruled blue photo mat to the bottom. Hide seams with paper ribbon wrapped around the back.

Continued

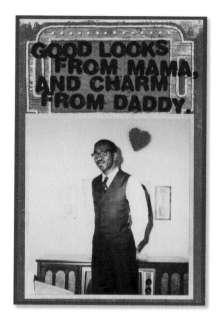

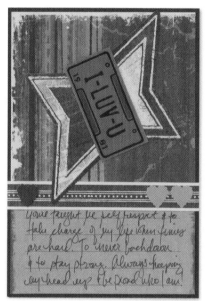

- Adhere 2 paper tags together, shaping a butterfly form. Affix a sticker on green photo mat. Trim to size and adhere to center of tags.
- Using the scallop Lovable Mini Pocket Punch and your choice of paper, embellish pages with hearts. Affix a few with Foam Squares to add dimension.

Spread 3

- On left side, adhere your choice of printed paper to background.
- Adhere a 4" x 6" photo to a cream photo mat. Trim excess, leaving a thin frame around photo, and adhere to page. Affix title sticker across photo.
- On right side, trim ½ inch of paper frame and adhere to top right of page. Cut ruled photo mat with Custom Cutting System and adhere behind trimmed paper frame. Adhere frame to left edge of page. Journal using Brown Dual-Tip Pen. Adhere paper tag to bottom center of page and affix title sticker.
- Using the scallop Lovable Mini Pocket Punch, embellish pages with hearts. Affix a few with Foam Squares to add dimension.

Spread 2

Spread 3

Spread 4

- On left side, adhere your choice of printed paper to background.
- Adhere 3³/₄" x 3³/₄" photo to blue 4" x 4" photo mat and adhere to page.
- Adhere a paper tag above top right of photo and affix title sticker.

- On right side, adhere a 4¼" x 6¼" from designer-print paper to background. Layer and adhere two paper tags. Handwrite journaling on tag and affix a title sticker.
- Using the Lovable Mini Pocket Punch, embellish both pages with hearts. Affix a few with Foam Squares to add dimension.

Spread 4

I LOVE YOU ALWAYS

12 x 12 page for a Magnetic Everyday Display

I ♥ YOU Always

I have loved you for nearly 20 years and still going very strong. I love you because you accept me for who I am, what I stand for even in the years of change and growth. As a military family we have gone through so much which has only made our relationship stronger and more enduring. I love you because when I am acting like a giggling 15 year old boy you are right there giggling with me and making sarcastic comments. I love you because you encourage me-always. I feel supported and loved 200% each day and each year.

I would never say that husbands aren't romantic. I will say that it might be easier to get your guy to show it if he could see a quick and uncomplicated way to do it! That's one of the best things about these Magnetic Everyday Displays. Put together something cute and special, add a few photos and display it today. Then change it up and say something different tomorrow. This project shows how easy it can be to say "I love you" in a way that will make any wife weak in the knees. You getting this, guys?!

Ingredients:

Weathered Chocolate Magnetic Everyday Display

8 x 8 Lovable Kit

Cheerful Valentine Additions

Brown Cardstock

White Swirly ABC/123 Stickers

Corner Maker

Personal Trimmer

12-inch Rotary Trimmer

Tape Runner

Instructions:

• Begin with a sheet of Brown Cardstock as a base.

• Trim a sheet of Lovable paper to a 6-inch square and adhere it to the upper-right corner of the cardstock.

• Adhere a $5\frac{1}{2}$" x 4" photo to a pink photo mat and adhere this to the left side of the page, as shown.

• Adhere a heart sticker to the lower-left corner of the photo, overlapping slightly.

• Trim a sheet of the phrases-patterned paper to 3" x $6\frac{1}{2}$."

• Trim a sheet of "XOXO" paper to $2\frac{3}{4}$" x $5\frac{3}{4}$" and adhere in the center of the phrases paper.

• Use the ABC stickers and spell "I...You Always," leaving space for a heart after "I."

• Layer 2 heart stickers and adhere beside the "I."

• Cut a $5\frac{1}{2}$" x $3\frac{1}{4}$" rectangle from the "XOXO" paper and use the Corner Maker on all four corners.

• Trim a pink photo mat to $4\frac{3}{4}$" x $2\frac{3}{4}$" and print or handwrite journaling onto this sheet. Use the Corner Maker on all 4 corners, then adhere it to the center of the red paper.

• Adhere a $3\frac{1}{2}$-inch heart border sticker along the top of the photo mat.

• Attach the photo mat with journaling to the Magnetic Everyday Display using the mini clothespins.

• Place 2 wallet-size photos to the left, hanging from the mini clothespins.

ALL ABOUT US

Album pages for a 12 x 12 scrapbook album

all about US

APPRECIATION

Joy

What is your full name?
Papa: William Francis Liebel, Jr.
Grammie: Susanne Ida Liebel

Did you have a nick name?
Papa: Bill
Grammie: Sue

When and where were you born?
Papa: May 1936 in Erie, PA
Grammie: January 1936 in Erie, PA

How did your family come to live there?
Papa: My Grandfather emigrated from Germany had
come over earlier.
Grammie: My Grandparents were immigrants in the late 1800's to live
with older siblings that and my Mom & Dad were born in Erie.

How did your mom & dad choose your name?
Papa: They named me after my father.
Grammie: I don't know how my name was chosen.

What did you want to be when you grew up?
Papa: Engineer
Grammie: I did not want to go to college just wanted to work in an office.
My first job paid $1.00 an hour and I thought that was great.

What is your earliest childhood memory?
Papa: Visiting my mother's sister and her family
(my cousins), who lived on a small far.
Grammie: Going to my Aunts and playing with my cousins who had
woods behind their house.

What kind of games did you play growing up?
Papa: Monopoly, Sorry and Chinese Checkers
Grammie: Games were mostly Monopoly and hide & seek in the summer.

What was your favorite toy and why?
Papa: Toy soldiers and army stuff.
Grammie: I always liked playing with dolls.

What was your favorite thing to do for fun?
Papa: Playing baseball with the neighbor kids (almost every day in the
summer) & go to the 25 cent double feature movies with a serial and a
cartoon on Sunday afternoons.
Grammie: Going to the beach when my Dad came home from work. He
always let us jump off his shoulders when we were younger.

What were your favorite foods?
Papa: Roast beef and mashed potatoes.
Grammie: Home cooked meals.

**What world events had the most impact on you while you were growing
up?**
Papa: World War II
Grammie: None I can think of at the moment.

Page 1

Looking for a gift that keeps on giving? How about some perspective! This is a great idea – especially for families who live far apart. "Interview" all of your family members and create a single book that can help kids understand who they are and where they fit in. Asking everyone the same set of standard questions makes the project more manageable.

Ingredients:

12 x 12 Coverset

12 x 12 Scrapbook Pages

Gratitude Paper & Photo Mat Pack

Gratitude Embellishment Pack

Gratitude Title Stickers

Espresso Cardstock

White Cardstock

Simple Brown ABC/123 Stickers

Simple Brown Monogram Stickers

Simple White ABC/123 Stickers

Simple White Monogram Stickers

All-Purpose Scissors

Corner Maker

Border Maker System (with Picket Fence and Scallop Stitch Cartridges)

Blossom Place 'n' Punch

Postage Stamp Place 'n' Punch

12-inch Rotary Trimmer

Foam Squares

Tape Runner

Precision Point Adhesive

Fonts: Calibri and Lucinda Calligraphy

Instructions:

Page 1

- Print or handwrite journaling onto White Cardstock and trim to 5″ x 11.″ Round the top- and bottom-right corners with your Corner Maker and adhere it to the right side of Espresso Cardstock, as shown.
- Cut a 6½″ x 11″ strip of orange-circle paper. Round top- and bottom-left corners with your Corner Maker and adhere it to the left of the journaling block.
- Cut a 1½″ x 11″ strip of brown designer-print paper and position it to cover the seam.
- Mat a 5″ x 7″ photo on a 5¼″ x 7¼″ piece of distressed-white paper. Round bottom-left of both photo and photo mat with your Corner Maker and adhere to bottom-left of page.
- Affix a paper tag on and above the left side of your photo and embellish with one green flower using the Blossom Place 'n' Punch. Add an epoxy sticker and title sticker.
- Affix monogram stickers (use Foam Squares under one letter) and ABC stickers to create your title.
- Embellish the top of journaling block with green and orange paper tags, tucked behind. Add a blue square paper tag to fit in the upper corner of the journaling block and embellish with a title sticker, Blossom Place 'n' Punch flower and epoxy sticker.

Continued

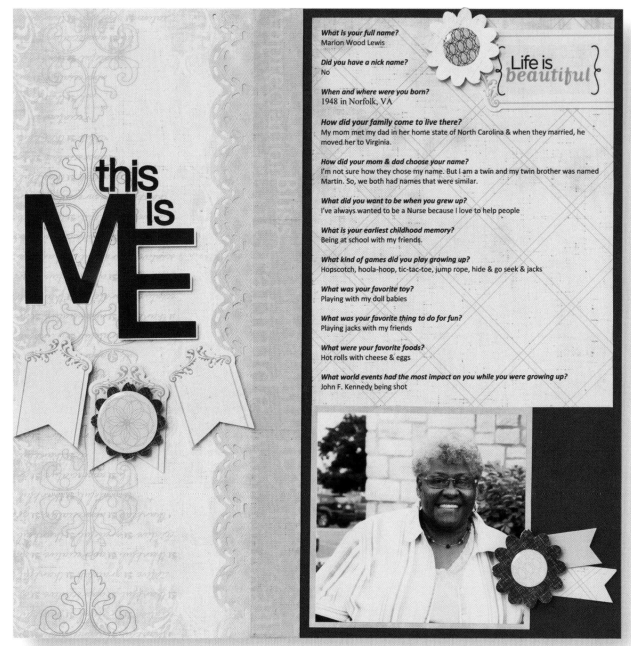

this is ME

What is your full name?
Marion Wood Lewis

Did you have a nick name?
No

When and where were you born?
1948 in Norfolk, VA

How did your family come to live there?
My mom met my dad in her home state of North Carolina & when they married, he moved her to Virginia.

How did your mom & dad choose your name?
I'm not sure how they chose my name. But I am a twin and my twin brother was named Martin. So, we both had names that were similar.

What did you want to be when you grew up?
I've always wanted to be a Nurse because I love to help people

What is your earliest childhood memory?
Being at school with my friends.

What kind of games did you play growing up?
Hopscotch, hoola-hoop, tic-tac-toe, jump rope, hide & go seek & jacks

What was your favorite toy?
Playing with my doll babies

What was your favorite thing to do for fun?
Playing jacks with my friends

What were your favorite foods?
Hot rolls with cheese & eggs

What world events had the most impact on you while you were growing up?
John F. Kennedy being shot

Life is *beautiful*

Page 2

Page 2

- Cut a 5½" x 12" strip of white-scroll paper and adhere it to the left edge of Espresso Cardstock.
- Using the Border Maker (Scallop Stitch Cartridge), punch two 1½" x 12" border strips of green paper. Layer them together and adhere them to the edge of the white scroll paper. Hide seams using blue paper ribbon.
- Print or handwrite journaling onto green paper, trim to 6" x 7½," and adhere it to the right side of page. In the top-right corner, adhere a paper tag and add a title sticker. Embellish with a Blossom Place 'n' Punch flower (using Foam Squares) and an epoxy sticker.
- Trim a green photo mat to 4½" x 4½" and mount a 4" x 4" photo. Adhere it below journaling as shown. Embellish the photo with 2 hand-cut tags and a brown Place 'n' Punch flower (using Foam Squares). Add an epoxy sticker on top.
- Cut 1 green and 2 blue paper tags in half, making angled cuts as shown. Use Foam Squares to adhere them on left side. Embellish center tag with Blossom Place 'n' Punch flower, adorned with an epoxy sticker.
- Affix title using monogram stickers and ABC stickers. Use Foam Squares to pop up part of the monogram E.

Page 3

- Adhere a 7" x 4½" rectangle of the brown-circle paper toward the top of the Espresso Cardstock background, as shown.
- Using the Border Maker (Picket Fence Cartridge), punch the bottom of blue paper and trim it to 1" x 11." Weave 11 inches of orange paper ribbon through slots and adhere it, centered, at the bottom of the page.
- Print or handwrite journaling onto White Cardstock, trim it to 11" x 5" and adhere it to the bottom of the page.
- Punch 2 picket fence border strips out of brown paper. Trim them to 1" x 11." Layer them together and adhere to the bottom edge of the brown-circle paper. Hide seams using a ½" x 11" strip of the green paper.
- Trim a photo mat to 4¼" x 4¼" and mount a 4" x 4" photo. Position it in the upper-left corner, as shown.
- Affix title using monogram stickers on the brown-circle paper. Print the first part of the title onto a blue photo mat, trim it to 1" x 4" and cut angled edges as shown. Cut an orange paper tag in half and adhere both pieces, slightly tucked behind the photo, as shown.
- Embellish the upper corner of the title area with an orange Postage Stamp Place 'n' Punch shape and adorn it with a square epoxy sticker.
- Affix title sticker to upper-right side of journaling block, as shown.

Continued

Interview with PAPA

What is your full name?
Isaiah Jeremiah Lewis

Did you have a nick name?
Short - for a long time, I stayed at 5' 2" & weighed 119 lbs, which seemed like I had stopped growing. It wasn't until after I came home from the Army, I grew 7 to 8 inches taller and gained 35 lbs.

When and where were you born?
February 1941 in Franklin, VA

How did your family come to live there?
My biological father moved met my mother in Rocky Mount, VA and moved to Franklin, VA where I was born. My mother is originally from Wilmington, NC. After my biological father left, she met my step-father while he was in the Navy and they built a life in Chesapeake, VA.

How did your mom & dad choose your name?
Parent wanted me to have biblical name & my last name is my mother's maiden name

What is your earliest childhood memory?
Walking to school with my mother and childhood friend every day in 1947 at Titustown Elementary

What did you want to be when you grew up?
A Pilot

What kind of games did you play growing up?
Playing marbles and hide & seek

What was your favorite toy?
1950's Lionel Train

What was your favorite thing to do for fun?
Hanging out with friends down at Wards Corner in Norfolk and street skating with friends

What were your favorite foods?
Black eyed peas, hamhock, crab, fish, chicken, collards & sweet potatoes

What world events had the most impact on you while you were growing up?
Watching war air planes fly over my neighborhood, heading over to fight the Korean War, watching Dodgers beat the Yankees in the World Series in 1955, the space shuttle landing on the moon, seeing Jesse Owens race in the track & field event to beat Hitler's team during the Olympics, Mohammad Ali becoming the World Champion in Boxing during the Olympics, fighting in the Vietnam War & to be alive during this time in my life when our country has its first African American President of the United States.

DELIGHT in the *little* THINGS

Page 3

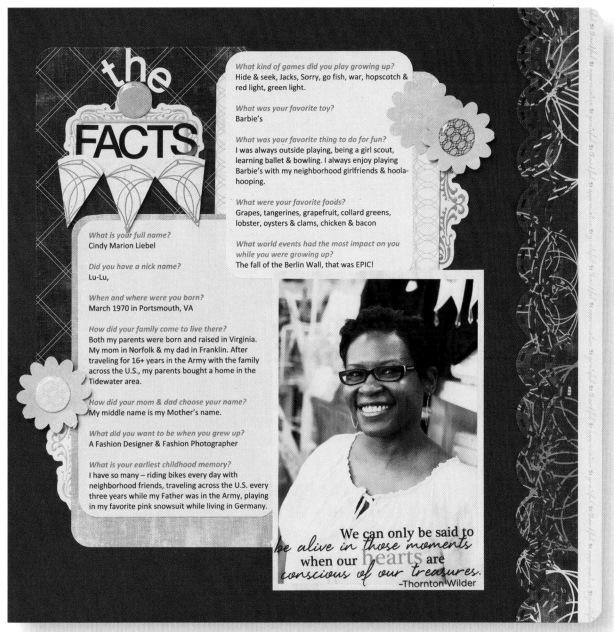

the FACTS

What kind of games did you play growing up?
Hide & seek, Jacks, Sorry, go fish, war, hopscotch & red light, green light.

What was your favorite toy?
Barbie's

What was your favorite thing to do for fun?
I was always outside playing, being a girl scout, learning ballet & bowling. I always enjoy playing Barbie's with my neighborhood girlfriends & hoola-hooping.

What were your favorite foods?
Grapes, tangerines, grapefruit, collard greens, lobster, oysters & clams, chicken & bacon

What world events had the most impact on you while you were growing up?
The fall of the Berlin Wall, that was EPIC!

What is your full name?
Cindy Marion Liebel

Did you have a nick name?
Lu-Lu,

When and where were you born?
March 1970 in Portsmouth, VA

How did your family come to live there?
Both my parents were born and raised in Virginia. My mom in Norfolk & my dad in Franklin. After traveling for 16+ years in the Army with the family across the U.S., my parents bought a home in the Tidewater area.

How did your mom & dad choose your name?
My middle name is my Mother's name.

What did you want to be when you grew up?
A Fashion Designer & Fashion Photographer

What is your earliest childhood memory?
I have so many – riding bikes every day with neighborhood friends, traveling across the U.S. every three years while my Father was in the Army, playing in my favorite pink snowsuit while living in Germany.

We can only be said to be alive in those moments when our hearts are conscious of our treasures.
-Thornton Wilder

Page 4

- Use the Corner Maker to round the right 2 corners of a sheet of Espresso Cardstock for your background.
- Round all 4 corners on one brown photo mat and adhere mat to the top-left corner of the page, as shown.
- Round the corners of a blue-and-white photo mat and adhere to the right side of the brown photo mat. Print or handwrite the last half of the journaling onto a distressed-white photo mat. Round all 4 corners and adhere it to the blue-and-white photo mat.
- Round the corners of an orange photo mat, overlap and adhere to the bottom of both the brown and the blue-and-white mats. Print the first half of your journaling onto a green photo mat, round all 4 corners and adhere it to the orange mat.
- Trim a distressed-white photo mat to $4\frac{1}{4}''$ x $6\frac{1}{4}''$ and add a 4" x 6" photo. Adhere it to the right side of the orange mat and bottom of blue-and-white mat. Affix a title sticker to the bottom of the photo.
- Use Border Maker (Scallop Stitch Cartridge) to punch 3 brown decorative $1\frac{1}{4}''$ x 12" border strips. Layer them and adhere across the left edge of the page. Use Corner Maker to round right corners.
- Adhere 12 inches of paper ribbon to the right edge of the page to hide seams and round corners.
- Cut half of a blue paper tag, adhere it to the brown photo mat, add a title using ABC stickers and adorn it with a round epoxy sticker in the center.

- Using the orange, round paper tag, cut triangles. Adhere them below the title to hide the seams of the paper tag, using Foam Squares.
- Embellish the top right of your journaling block with a paper tag and 2 Blossom Place 'n' Punch flowers, 1 using Foam Squares and an epoxy sticker.
- Embellish the bottom left of your journaling block with a paper tag and 1 Blossom Place 'n' Punch flower (using Foam Squares). Adorn with an epoxy sticker.

Page 5

- Cut a $6\frac{1}{2}''$ x 10" rectangle from brown designer-print paper. Adhere it to a sheet of Espresso Cardstock.
- Using your Border Maker (Picket Fence Cartridge), punch a sheet of orange paper, cut off a 1" x 10" border strip and adhere it on the right edge of your brown rectangle. Hide seams using 10 inches of paper ribbon.
- Cut a $1\frac{1}{2}''$ x 10" strip of distressed-white paper. Round top- and bottom-left corners with Corner Maker and place it to the left of your brown rectangle.
- Use Border Maker (Picket Fence Cartridge) to punch the edge of the brown-circle paper. Cut a 1" x 10" border and adhere it across the distressed-white paper. Hide seams using 10 inches of orange paper ribbon.
- Print or handwrite journaling onto a $4\frac{1}{4}''$ x $7\frac{1}{4}''$ rectangle of the green cross-hatch paper. Round corners and adhere it to the center of the page.
- Trim a photo mat to $6\frac{1}{4}''$ x $4\frac{1}{4}''$ and add a 6" x 4"

Continued

What is your full name?
Timothy John Liebel

Did you have a nick name?
Timmy

When and where were you born?
April 1970 in Erie, PA

How did your family come to live there?
My grandparent immigrated from Germany to Erie where my parents were born.

How did your mom & dad choose your name?
I'm not sure.

What did you want to be when you grew up?
An Astronaut

What is your earliest childhood memory?
In 1976, it was the United States 200th Anniversary and I remember painting fire hydrants patriotic colors in my neighborhood.

What kind of games did you play growing up?
Mostly Monopoly

What was your favorite toy?
Stretch Armstrong man

What was your favorite thing to do for fun?
Playing outside with my friends

What were your favorite foods?
Chicken & biscuits

What world events had the most impact on you while you were growing up?
Space shuttle Challenger exploding.

Q&A

Page 5

photo. Adhere it to the bottom center of page, below the journaling block.

- Embellish journaling block with epoxy stickers in the upper-right corner.
- Add the green paper tag. Adhere the circular title sticker above the right edge of your photo, as shown. Adhere the rectangular epoxy sticker. Finish off with a title using the ABC stickers.

Page 6

- Adhere a 1″ x 12″ strip of distressed-white paper across the bottom edge of a sheet of Espresso Cardstock. Top that with a ½″ x 12″ strip of green-circle paper.
- Adhere a 2″ x 12″ strip of blue-circle paper across the top edge of the page.
- Using your Border Maker (Picket Fence Cartridge), punch out three 1½″ x 12″ border strips of green circle paper, layer them together and adhere them below the blue-circle paper. Hide seams using blue paper ribbon.
- Cut the brown paper tag in half and adhere it in the upper-left corner, above the paper ribbon. Embellish it with an orange postage stamp using the Postage Stamp Place 'n' Punch. Add a square epoxy sticker.
- Use ABC stickers to add a title across the paper ribbon.
- Print or handwrite journaling onto blue paper and trim it to 7″ x 8¼″. Tuck it slightly under the decorative border at top and adhere it to the page. Affix a long

title sticker to hide bottom seams of journaling block.

- Trim a photo mat to 4¼″ x 6¼″ and add a 4″ x 6″ photo. Adhere it to the bottom-right side of the journaling block, just above the long title sticker.
- Adhere a paper tag and title sticker to the layout. Adhere an epoxy sticker to an orange postage stamp cut with your Postage Stamp Place 'n' Punch and affix it to the right end of the paper tag.

Tip: If you want to create the same project in less time, simply use the photos and interview questions, and adhere them to an album page. Fast and still fab!

Back in the Day...

find the joy in life

What is your full name?
Isaiah Jeremiah Lewis, Jr.

Did you have a nick name?
Izzy

When and where were you born?
November 1970 in Bad Kreuenach, Rheinland Pflaz, Germany

How did your family come to live there?
My father was stationed in the Army at the time I was born. My family's home is in the Tidewater area in Virginia.

How did your mom & dad choose your name?
Was named after my dad

What did you want to be when you grew up?
A Fireman, Policeman or Construction worker

What is your earliest childhood memory?
Singing the happy birthday song at my 5th birthday party while living in Kentucky

What kind of games did you play growing up?
Sorry & baseball

What was your favorite toy?
Star Wars figures & battleships & GI Joe

What was your favorite thing to do for fun?
Hide & Seek and picking on my sisters friends

What were your favorite foods?
French friends & hamburgers

What world events had the most impact on you while you were growing up?
The 1991 war in Kuwait; I had just turned 18 and was afraid I was going to be drafted and fight in the war.

grateful ❧ thankful ❧ appreciative ❧ grateful ❧ thankful ❧ appreciative ❧ grateful ❧ thankful ❧ appreciative ❧ grateful ❧ thankful ❧ appreciative ❧ grateful ❧ thankful ❧ appreciative ❧ grateful ❧ thankful

Page 6

Digital layout for an 11 x 8½ Photo Panel

I Am Thankful For...

Whoever it was who picked up the papers off the table and took out the trash.

Thanks Mystery Boy!!

A Digital Photo Panel makes an exceptional gift – easy, personal, affordable. Basically, your digital image is printed directly on the panel. With no "frame," you're free to digitally create using the full space. In this case, we've created a frame with a blank center space on which you can write a handwritten message of gratitude and change it with new ones (using a dry-erase marker). This would make an amazing gift for a spouse or for a dear friend.

Ingredients:

StoryBook Creator 4.0 Software

Gratitude Series Digital Kit

Font: HandTIMES

Instructions:

• Create an 8.5 x 11" landscape Photo Panel project.

• Add a strip of Paper 16 to the left side of the project.

• Add Paper 17 next to it, covering most of the project.

• Add a strip of the Blue Ribbon along the bottom of the project.

• Add an 8" x 7" white rectangle to the center of the project.

• Cut out the orange part of Paper 19 and add it to the left side of the project.

• Under the Cut & Fill tab, select straight-shaped edge-arch. Delete the unwanted area to create the border edge.

• Add a strip of Cream Ribbon next to the open scalloped edge. Cut a thin strip from Paper 21 and add it on top of the Blue Ribbon at the bottom.

• Add a Blue Frame to the top left of the project.

• Add a photo to the center of the frame.

• Add a title in brown across the top of the project.

• Add a drop shadow to everything.

• Upload and print your project at digital. creativememories.com.

"I HOPE" CALENDAR

Digital layouts for an 8 x 12 calendar

LAST YEAR'S SNOW WAS SUCH A FUN AND UNEXPECTED SURPRISE! I HOPE WE HAVE SNOW AGAIN THIS YEAR!

January 2012

Sunday	Monday	Tuesday	Wednesda	Thursday	Friday	Saturday
1	2	3	4	5	6	7
8	9	10	11	12	13	14
15	16	17	18	19	20	21
22	23	24	25	26	27	28
29	30	31				

Ingredients:

StoryBook Creator 4.0 Software

Reflections Digital Power® Palette

Font: Bank Gothic

Instructions:

Create a new 8 x 12 calendar project.

January

• Add Paper 26 as a background to the page and Paper 40 behind the calendar.

• Cut a rectangle from Paper 1 and add it to the left side of the page.

• Cut a rectangle from Paper 30 and add next to Paper 1.

• Cut a punched edge into this paper.

• Add Ribbon 4 over the seam between these papers.

• Cut a large rectangle out of Paper 40 and add to the center of the page.

• Add Ribbon 7 to the bottom of the rectangle.

• Add a photo above the ribbon.

• Add the flowers to the upper-left side of the photo mat.

• Add journaling to the bottom of the layout.

• Add a drop shadow to everything except the journaling.

*Talk about your everyday gifts! A custom calendar is a beautiful, personal way to keep everyone organized. But my favorite part of this project is the way that we've infused hope into every month. Every day your family is greeted by smiling photos of themselves **and** a gentle reminder of your hopes and wishes for the coming year! (Want to make a project like this really easy? You can download **free** templates from creativememories.com.)*

DAD LOVED THE VALENTINE YOU MADE HIM THIS YEAR TY! I HOPE YOU WON'T GROW OUT OF MAKING US HANDMADE VALENTINES ANY TIME SOON! I LOVE TO SEE HOW YOUR READING AND WRITING IS DEVELOPING!

February 2012

	Sunday	Monday	Tuesday	Wednesda	Thursday	Friday	Saturday
				1	2	3	4
	5	6	7	8	9	10	11
	12	13	14	15	16	17	18
	19	20	21	22	23	24	25
	26	27	28	29			

February

- Add Paper 11 as a background to the page and add Paper 1 behind the calendar, with opacity lowered to 50 percent.
- Cut a rectangle out of Paper 37 and add to the left side of the layout. Round the corners of this paper.
- Cut a small rectangle out of Paper 39 and add on the right side of the page. Round the corners and then add journaling.
- Add photo to the left side of the page and round the corners.
- Add Ribbon 7 and Ribbon 8 across the bottom of the photo.
- Add leaf embellishment to the bottom-left corner of the photo.
- Add a drop shadow to everything except the journaling.

> **How to apply drop shadows**
> *Select all layers while holding the shift key (except the journaling and title). Under the Format tab, apply a heavy or light shadow.*

Continued

I ADORE THIS PHOTO OF YOU BLAKE! I
ADORE THE WAY YOU WERE STUDYING THE
ARRIVAL OF SPRING THOUGH YOUR WINDOW. I
HOPE THAT YOU WILL ALWAYS MARVEL AT THE
BEAUTY IN BLOOM ALL AROUND YOU!

life is beautiful

March 2012

	Sunday	Monday	Tuesday	Wednesda	Thursday	Friday	Saturday
					1	2	3
	4	5	6	7	8	9	10
	11	12	13	14	15	16	17
	18	19	20	21	22	23	24
	25	26	27	28	29	30	31

March

- Add Paper 5 as a background and add Paper 42 behind the calendar.
- Cut a large scalloped circle out of Paper 41 and arrange it so it's hanging off the left side of the page.
- Cut a circle from Paper 44 and center it over the scalloped circle.
- Add Ribbon 7 across the lower-left side of the page.
- Cut a rectangle out of Paper 38 and add it near the center of the page.
- Add a photo over the rectangle, cut from Paper 38.
- Add Circle Tag 1, flowers and title as shown around the bottom of the photo.
- Add journaling to the top of the circle.
- Add a drop shadow to everything except the journaling.

GOING ON A FAMILY OUTING TO SEE THE TEXAS BLUEBONNETS IS ALWAYS A FUN DAY! I AM CONSTANTLY AMAZED AT THE CHANGE A FEW SHORT WEEKS CAN MAKE. WINTER DISAPPEARS AND SUDDENLY SPRING IS BURSTING ALL AROUND. THIS YEAR I WAS ALSO MARVELING AT THE CLOSENESS THE TWO OF YOU BOYS HAVE BEEN SHARING LATELY! YOU HAVE BECOME SUCH GOOD FRIENDS AND BUDDIES FOR EACH OTHER! I HOPE THAT AS THE REST OF THIS YEAR GOES BY YOU CONTINUE TO GROW CLOSE BOTH AS BROTHERS AND AS GOOD FRIENDS!

April 2012

Sunday	Monday	Tuesday	Wednesda	Thursday	Friday	Saturday
1	2	3	4	5	6	7
8	9	10	11	12	13	14
15	16	17	18	19	20	21
22	23	24	25	26	27	28
29	30					

April

- Add Paper 12 as a background to the page and add Paper 25 behind the calendar.
- Cut a rectangle out of Paper 43 and add to the top of the page.
- Cut a rectangle out of Paper 44. Add it across the top of the page. Under the Cut & Fill tab, cut a punched edge.
- Add Ribbon 7 across the seam.
- Cut a rectangle out of Paper 21 and add it to the left side of the page.
- Add a photo over this paper.
- Add Circle Tag 6 to the lower-left side of the page.
- Add Ribbon 8 to the left side of the page.
- Add 2 flowers to the bottom left side of the page.
- Add journaling to the left side of the page.
- Add a drop shadow to everything except the journaling.

Continued

I JUST LOVE THE MOTHER'S DAY PROJECTS YOU MADE AT SCHOOL TY! YOU WERE SO SECRETIVE ABOUT WHAT YOU HAD BEEN MAKING, AND IT WAS A VERY NICE SURPRISE THAT MORNING TO SEE YOU FINALLY UNVEIL ALL THE ARTWORK YOU WORKED ON SO HARD AT SCHOOL! I LOVED IT ALL AND I HOPE THAT YOU DON'T GROW OUT OF MAKING HANDMADE MOTHER'S DAY GIFTS ANYTIME SOON!

HAPPY DAY!

May

- Add Paper 4 as a background and add Paper 9 behind the calendar.
- Add Ribbon 7 along the bottom of the page.
- Cut a rectangle out of Paper 22 and add it to the left side of the page.
- Add a photo on top of Paper 22.
- Add a leaf embellishment to the lower-right corner of the photo.
- Add Decorative Tag 6 to the bottom-right side of the page, then add a title sticker to this tag.
- Add journaling to the middle-right side of the page.
- Add a drop shadow to everything except the journaling and title embellishment.

May 2011

	Sunday	Monday	Tuesday	Wednesda	Thursday	Friday	Saturday
	1	2	3	4	5	6	7
	8	9	10	11	12	13	14
	15	16	17	18	19	20	21
	22	23	24	25	26	27	28
	29	30	31				

You were so cute at your pre-school graduation Blake! I hope this is the start of many good years of education for you, and I look forward to all the graduations to come!

	Sunday	Monday	Tuesday	Wednesda	Thursday	Friday	Saturday
						1	2
	3	4	5	6	7	8	9
	10	11	12	13	14	15	16
	17	18	19	20	21	22	23
	24	25	26	27	28	29	30

June 2012

June

- Add Paper 1 as a background to the page and add Paper 27 behind the calendar.
- Cut a rectangle out of Paper 22 and add it to the top of the page.
- Cut a punched edge along the bottom of this paper.
- Add Ribbon 4 across the top of the layout, next to the punched edge.
- Cut a rectangle out of Paper 30 and add it to the lower-right side of the page.
- Cut a rectangle from Paper 38 and add it to the right side of the page.
- Add a photo on top of the rectangle made from Paper 38.
- Add Ribbon 1 across the bottom of the photo.
- Add Scallop Tag 4 to the left side of the page.
- Add journaling to the tag.
- Add a leaf and flower embellishment to the lower left side of the photo.
- Add a drop shadow to everything except the journaling.

Continued

CELEBRATING THE 4TH OF JULY IS NEVER COMPLETE WITHOUT GOING TO THE PARADE. YOU BOYS LOVE TO WAVE YOUR FLAGS AND CATCH CANDY AND I LOVE TO EXPLAIN TO YOU THE LOVE YOUR DADDY AND I HAVE FOR OUR COUNTRY. I HOPE VERY MUCH THAT YOU WILL GROW UP TO HAVE THAT SAME LOVE AND SENSE OF PATRIOTISM!

July 2012

	Sunday	Monday	Tuesday	Wednesda	Thursday	Friday	Saturday
		1	2	3	4	5	6	7
	8	9	10	11	12	13	14
	15	16	17	18	19	20	21
	22	23	24	25	26	27	28
	29	30	31				

July

- Add Paper 3 as a background to the page and add Paper 38 behind the calendar.
- Cut a large rectangle out of Paper 27 and add it to the center of the page.
- Cut a tall rectangle out of Paper 37 and add it to the left side of the page, then give it a punched edge.
- Add Ribbon 8 over the seam between these 2 papers.
- Cut a rectangle out of Paper 30 and add it to the lower-right corner of the page.
- Add a photo on top of Paper 30.
- Add Ribbon 7 across the bottom of the page.
- Add a leaf embellishment to the lower-left corner of the photo.
- Add journaling to the top of the page.
- Add a drop shadow to everything except the journaling.

OH HOW YOU BOYS LOVE WATERMELON! WE BUY TOO MANY TO COUNT EACH SUMMER IN AN ATTEMPT TO TRY AND KEEP YOU ALL SATISFIED! WE ARE LUCKY ENOUGH THAT WE CAN OFTEN BUY THEM STRAIGHT FROM LOCAL FARMERS AND THEY ARE OH SO JUICY AND GOOD! I HOPE THAT THIS IS A PLEASURE WE CAN INDULGE IN FREQUENTLY IN ALL THE SUMMER'S TO COME!

August 2012

Sunday	Monday	Tuesday	Wednesda	Thursday	Friday	Saturday
			1	2	3	4
5	6	7	8	9	10	11
12	13	14	15	16	17	18
19	20	21	22	23	24	25
26	27	28	29	30	31	

August

- Add Paper 10 as a background to the page and add Paper 3 behind the calendar.
- Cut a large rectangle out of Paper 22 and add it to the center of the page.
- Add a photo to the top of Paper 22.
- Add Ribbon 1 across the bottom of the page.
- Add Circle Tag 1 to the lower-left corner of the page.
- Add 2 flower embellishments to the tag.
- Add the title embellishment to the upper-left corner of the page.
- Add journaling beneath the photo.
- Add a drop shadow to everything except the journaling and title embellishment.

Continued

LAST YEAR WAS A
GREAT SCHOOL YEAR
FOR YOU TY! I HOPE
THIS YEAR YOU HAVE
ANOTHER GREAT
TEACHER, AND
CONTINUE TO EXCEL
IN YOUR CLASS!

September 2012

Sunday	Monday	Tuesday	Wednesda	Thursday	Friday	Saturday
						1
2	3	4	5	6	7	8
9	10	11	12	13	14	15
16	17	18	19	20	21	22
23	24	25	26	27	28	29
30						

September

- Add Paper 7 as a background to the page and add Paper 41 behind the calendar.
- Cut a large rectangle from Paper 38 and add to the bottom of the page.
- Add Ribbon 4 across the seam between the background papers.
- Cut a rectangle out of Paper 41 and add it to the center of the page.
- Add a photo to the center of Paper 41.
- Add Rectangle Tag 5 to the right side of the page.
- Add journaling to the tag.
- Add a leaf embellishment to the lower-left side of the page.
- Add a drop shadow to everything except the journaling.

It's the little moments that make life big.

LAST YEAR WE DISCOVERED
HOW MUCH FUN IT IS TO
PRINT PUMPKIN CARVING
DESIGNS FROM THE
INTERNET. I HOPE WE HAVE
TIME TO DO THIS AGAIN THIS
HALLOWEEN! IT WAS SO
MUCH FUN THIS YEAR WE
MAY JUST HAVE TO MAKE A
TRADITION OUT OF IT!

October 2012

	Sunday	Monday	Tuesday	Wednesda	Thursday	Friday	Saturday
		1	2	3	4	5	6
	7	8	9	10	11	12	13
	14	15	16	17	18	19	20
	21	22	23	24	25	26	27
	28	29	30	31			

October

- Add Paper 24 as a background to the page and add Paper 28 behind the calendar.
- Cut a long rectangle out of Paper 12 and add it across the middle of the page.
- Cut a long rectangle from Paper 41 and add it across the center of the page.
- Add Ribbon 7 across the center of the page.
- Cut a rectangle out of Paper 28 and add it across the center of the page.
- Cut a rectangle out of Paper 1 and add it to the top of the page.
- Add a photo to the lower-left corner of the paper.
- Add Ribbon 8 across the lower-right side of the page.
- Add journaling to the lower-right side of the page.
- Add a flower and title embellishment to the page.
- Add a drop shadow to everything except the journaling and title embellishment.

Continued

I LOVE THE WAY FALL IS FILLED WITH BIRTHDAY'S IN OUR FAMILY! THERE IS ALWAYS SOME NEW CELEBRATION TO PLAN AND LOOK FORWARD TO! I HOPE THAT THIS YEAR BRINGS MANY MORE GOOD TIMES AS WE CELEBRATE THE VERY SPECIAL DAYS EACH OF YOU JOINED OUR FAMILY!

	Sunday	Monday	Tuesday	Wednesda	Thursday	Friday	Saturday
					1	2	3
	4	5	6	7	8	9	10
	11	12	13	14	15	16	17
	18	19	20	21	22	23	24
	25	26	27	28	29	30	

November 2012

November

- Add Paper 43 as a background to the page and add Paper 32 behind the calendar.
- Cut a small rectangle out of Paper 1 and add it to the left side of the page.
- Add a photo next to the rectangle.
- Cut a rectangle out of Paper 27 and add it to the right side of the layout.
- Cut a long rectangle out of Paper 28 and add it to the bottom of the layout, then give it an open-scalloped decorative edge.
- Add Ribbon 7 to the top and bottom of the page.
- Add Circle Tag 2 to the lower-right side of the page.
- Add journaling to the right side of the page.
- Add a drop shadow to everything except the journaling.

{capture} the moment

FOR MANY WEEKS LAST DECEMBER ALL I HEARD ABOUT WAS HOW MUCH YOU BOYS WANTED LEGOS FOR CHRISTMAS! I TEASED YOU RELENTLESSLY ABOUT HOW SANTA CLAUSE WAS OUT OF THEM AND THAT YOU WOULDN'T BE GETTING ANY THIS YEAR BECAUSE OF THE "LEGO SHORTAGE." LUCKILY FOR THE TWO OF YOU, SANTA FOUND SOME SOMEWHERE AND YOU WERE BOTH SO EXCITED AND GRATEFUL FOR YOUR FUN NEW SET. I HOPE NEXT YEAR YOU ARE JUST AS EXCITED ON CHRISTMAS MORNING!

December 2012

Sunday	Monday	Tuesday	Wednesda	Thursday	Friday	Saturday
						1
2	3	4	5	6	7	8
9	10	11	12	13	14	15
16	17	18	19	20	21	22
23	24	25	26	27	28	29
30	31					

December
- Add Paper 11 as a background to the page and add Paper 1 behind the calendar, with the opacity lowered to about 50 percent.
- Cut a long rectangle out of Paper 43 and add it to the left side of the page.
- Cut a long rectangle out of Paper 28 and add it to the left side of the layout, then give it a scalloped decorative edge.
- Add Ribbon 7 over the seam.
- Cut a small rectangle out of Paper 23 and add it to the left side of the page.
- Add a photo on top of Paper 23 and add Rectangle Tag 3 to the right side of the page.
- Add flower and leaf embellishments to the upper-right and lower-left sides of the page.
- Add a title embellishment to the tag.
- Add the journaling to the bottom of the page.
- Add a drop shadow to everything except the journaling.

HOSTESS THANK YOU

8 x 8 page for a Mini Magnetic Everyday Display

This idea makes me smile every time. How do you say thank you to a host? A thank-you gift? A thank-you note? For this project, we've taken the two and smooshed them together brilliantly. Decorate the display and add a sweet little note of thanks. Plus, Aunt Jeannie and Uncle Bill are left with a Mini Magnetic Everyday Display they can use for years to showcase what's new.

Ingredients:

Mini Magnetic Everyday Display

Gratitude Mini Display Accents

Foam Squares

Tape Runner

Tip:

For great ideas on how to present this gift to your hostesses, look to Chapter 4.

Instructions:

- Add the multi-patterned paper as a base for the project.
- Adhere a 4″ x 6″ photo.
- Print or handwrite journaling on light-colored paper and cut out, saving a thin area on the right side to add a quarter-inch strip of brown-patterned paper from the reverse side. Adhere to page using Foam Squares.
- Add embellishment to upper-left corner with Foam Squares.
- Add title accent to display with mini clothespins.

GROW WITH ME (AND THE TREE)

Album pages for a 4 x 6 PicFolio® Album

*So much of life goes flying by at a pace that makes your hair flutter. But many of the really important things move a bit slower. (And you definitely don't want to miss them!) This idea is a fun little reinterpretation of the old tick marks on the doorframe. It makes a wonderful, thoughtful little gift for the mom of a growing toddler. Give it on a child's birthday along with a small seedling or sapling tree so she can start taking annual pictures to see who grows faster! It's a cute way to track growth **and** start building some ties to nature and conservation!*

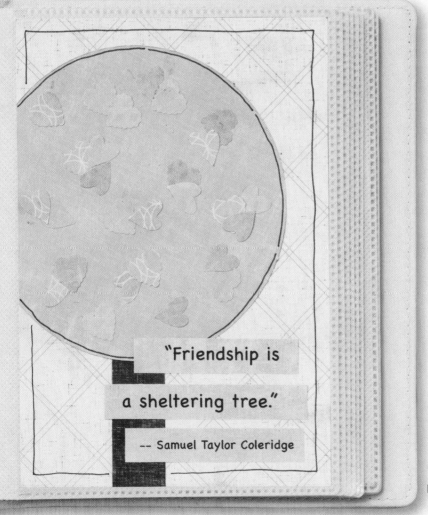

"Friendship is

a sheltering tree."

-- Samuel Taylor Coleridge

Intro Page

Ingredients:

4 x 6 PicFolio® Album

Gratitude Paper & Photo Mat Pack

Simple Brown ABC/123 Stickers

Brown Dual-Tip Pen

Lovable Mini Pocket Punches

Personal Trimmer

Custom Cutting System
  (with Circle Patterns)

Precision Point Adhesive

Tape Runner

"He who plants a tree,

plants a hope."

– Lucy Larcom

Sophie,
We plan to
delight in
watching you
grow with the
tree. As you
nurture it, we
will nurture you.
Love you – Mom & Dad

2011

Sophie: Age 6 3ft. 11in. Sapling 2ft. 6in.

Spread 1

Instructions:

Intro Page:

- Use a cream patterned photo mat as a base.
- Cut a strip of brown paper to measure $\frac{3}{4}''$ x 2" inches. Adhere it to the paper as shown.
- Cut a circle from a green photo mat with the outside of the small circle pattern and the blue blade. Adhere it to the cream paper as shown. Trim the paper that hangs off the edge.
- Using the Lovable Mini Pocket Punches, punch several hearts from the green and orange papers and adhere them to the tree, randomly.
- Print your journaling on the blue photo mat. Cut it into strips and adhere it to the page as shown.
- Use the Brown Dual-Tip Pen to doodle along the edge of the tree, as well as the edge of the photo mat.

Continued

Spread 1:

- Use a cream patterned photo mat as a base for this page.
- Cut a strip of brown paper to measure $\frac{3}{4}$" x $2\frac{1}{4}$" and adhere it to the page as shown.
- Cut a circle from a green photo mat with the inside of the large circle pattern and the red blade. Adhere it to the cream paper as shown.
- Using the Lovable Mini Pocket Punches, punch several hearts from the green and orange papers and adhere them to the tree, randomly.
- Cut a piece of orange paper to measure $2\frac{1}{4}$" x 1." Add ABC stickers. Attach the orange piece to a piece of blue paper measuring $2\frac{3}{4}$" x $1\frac{1}{2}$" and adhere that to the page as shown.
- Print or handwrite journaling on the blue photo mat. Cut it into strips and adhere it to the page as shown.
- Using the Brown Dual-Tip Pen, doodle around the edges of the tree and the photo mat as shown.

"Plant trees. They give us two of the most crucial elements for our survival: oxygen and books."
– Whitney Brown

2013

Place Photo Here

Sophie: Tree:

All other spreads:

• Repeat the instructions for 2011, only make the brown paper longer so that the tree will show "growth."

Continue adding "years" to fill all the album pages. Place a photo next to each year to show how both the child and the tree have grown. Don't forget to fill in the height of the child and the tree.

TODAY'S MENU

Digital layout for a 12 x 12 Photo Panel

I love this simple idea for the gourmets on your gift list. A Photo Panel is a quick project you put together digitally. You can make one using gorgeous, free online templates at digital.creativememories.com or by using Creative Memories software. It can include photos, designs, quotes, journaling... but this idea doesn't use any photos at all. It takes advantage of the fact that a dry erase marker wipes cleanly off the Photo Panel material. So by including a white background, we've made a cute little bistro-style menu board that looks great in any kitchen.

Ingredients:

StoryBook Creator 4.0 Software

Nancy O'Dell Digital Recipe Kit

Rugged Outdoors Digital Alpha Set

Font: Pea Cathi

Instructions:

- Create a new 12 x 12 Photo Panel project.
- Add Paper 13 as a background to the project.
- Add a 1½" x 10¼" piece of Paper 3 to the left side of the project.
- Add a 9¾" x 9¼" white rectangle to the center.
- Add tape embellishment stickers to each of the corners, rotating so each will cover the corners.
- Add a line embellishment to the left side of the project. Add the spoons embellishment to the lower-right side of the project.
- Add "A Favorite Recipe" circle to the upper-left side.
- Add title with the Rugged Outdoors Alpha Set in black and the Pea Cathi font in teal to the top of the project.
- Add a drop shadow to everything except the word "Menu."

Milestone Gifts

My father-in-law recently celebrated his 80th birthday, and if that's not a milestone I don't know what is. So the family and I made a special gratitude album for him. He loved it. He really did. He read it, cover to cover, and showed it off to everyone. I think it truly touched him.

But just as exciting is what we got out of making the album. The time we spent sifting through old photos and talking about all those great stories made us feel closer to Papa Z than ever before. My husband told me afterward that it made him appreciate all over again what a great man his dad is. That's something I'll treasure as much as Papa Z treasures his album.

Weddings, births, milestone anniversaries and birthdays... These recipes can give you some tasty little ideas for celebrating those special, personal moments.

Chapter 2 Recipes

MESSAGES FOR THE NEW COUPLE

Album pages for an 8 x 8 scrapbook album

· Ted & Emily ·

est. 2011

May today be the happiest day of your lives.

Enjoy this guestbook filled with happiness from your
family and friends. Read it often and smile.

You are loved by every one of us here today
sharing in your joy.

Page 1

By adding some photos and idea starters, this gorgeous little 8 x 8 album puts a personal spin on the old wedding reception guest book. The pages ask simple, specific questions that will lead to real, honest, fun, heartwarming answers when the couple puts the album out at the reception for guests to fill in. No more "best wishes!" This will be one of the best gifts the couple receives ... and lots of fun for the guests as well.

Ingredients:

8 x 8 Coverset

8 x 8 White Scrapbook Pages

Reflections Power® Palette

Black Cardstock

White Cardstock

White Shimmer Cardstock

Black Simple Monogram Stickers

White Simple Monogram Stickers

Lovable Mini Pocket Punches

Destination Mini Pocket Punches

Circle Maker

Corner Maker

Puzzle Maker

Square Maker

Sweet Heart Maker

Tag Maker

All-Purpose Scissors

Creative Cuts Tool (with Distressing Tip)

Scallop Tearing Tool

12-inch Rotary Trimmer

Border Maker System (with Frame Chain and Picket Fence Cartridges)

Custom Cutting System (with Circle and Oval Patterns)

Foam Squares

Precision Point Adhesive

Tape Runner

Fonts: Lobster, Emmascript and Century Gothic

Instructions:

Page 1

• Trim White Shimmer Cardstock to 8″ x 8″ and use as base.

• Print or handwrite journaling on White Shimmer Cardstock, leaving space for the photo.

• Crop photo to 4″ x 3″ and round the corners. Adhere.

• Punch a large circle of blue patterned paper. Use the Sweet Heart Maker to punch a heart from the White Shimmer Cardstock. Adhere the heart to the circle, then place on the photo as shown.

Continued

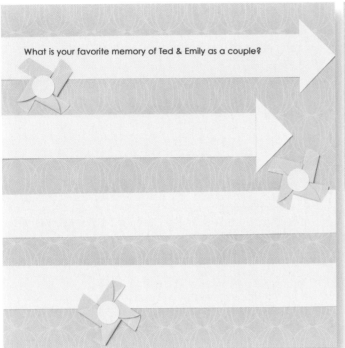

What is your favorite memory of Ted & Emily as a couple?

YOU & ME

LOVE

1st two-page spread

- Trim blue patterned paper to 12″ x 8.″ Then cut 4 inches off one edge.
- Adhere the 4-inch piece to the left side of an 8″ x 8″ piece of White Cardstock.
- Crop photo to 5½″ x 7½.″ Adhere as shown.
- Add the "You & Me" and "Love" stickers.
- Print or handwrite the journaling question on White Cardstock. Trim to 7″ x 1.″ Trim 3 more 1-inch White Cardstock strips. Cut them to varying lengths: approximately 6″, 8½″ and 8.″ Adhere them evenly on the left side of the spread, crossing to the right side for the 8½-inch strip.
- Punch 2 smaller squares with the Square Maker. Cut them in half, diagonally, and adhere 1 square to each journaling strip as an arrow.
- Punch 5 large circles from the green-patterned paper. Use scissors to snip them evenly in 4 places, making sure not to cut all the way through the circle. Fold the left corner of each pie-shaped wedge to the center and crease slightly to keep it in place. Place a period from the letter stickers over the center to hold it in place.
- Adhere the circular pinwheels as shown.

What is
your silliest
memory of
Ted & Emily?

laughter

Spread 2

2nd two-page spread

- Trim patterned paper to 12″ x 8.″ Cut off a 4″ x 8″ piece and adhere it to the left side of an 8″ x 8″ piece of White Cardstock. Crop photo to 4″ x 8″ and adhere to the right.
- Cut ½-inch strips of the green patterned paper. Position them as shown.
- Cut 8 White Cardstock circles using the inside of the medium Circle Pattern and the red blade.

- Place the circles on the green strips and adhere.
- Print or handwrite your journaling on White Cardstock. Trim and adhere.
- Punch 4 blue circles and 1 green circle with the smaller punch and 2 larger green circles with the larger punch. Adhere as shown.
- Punch 4 white hearts and adhere on the circles.
- Adhere a 1″ x 8″ green strip over the edge of the photo.
- Add the "Laughter" sticker.

Continued

Spread 3

3rd two-page spread

- Trim 2 sheets of White Shimmer Cardstock to 8" x 8."
- Crop photo to 5½" x 8" and adhere to the left side of the spread. Add the "Life is Beautiful" sticker.
- Trim the green patterned paper to 7" x 8" and adhere to the right side of the spread.
- Cut 6 ovals from White Cardstock, using the inside of the medium Oval Pattern and the blue blade. Cut a Black Cardstock mat and 2 gray photo mats with the green blade.

- Place the ovals as shown. Adhere.
- Use the Destination Mini Pocket Punch to punch 2 cars from the Black Cardstock.
- Use Foam Squares to adhere the 2 punched cars.

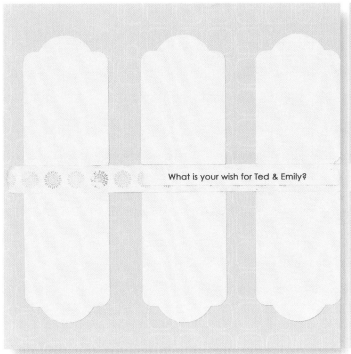

What is your wish for Ted & Emily?

Spread 4

4th two-page spread

- Trim green patterned paper to 12″ x 8.″ Cut off a 4″ x 8″ piece and adhere it to the left side of an 8″ x 8″ piece of White Shimmer Cardstock. Crop photo to 4″ x 8″ and adhere to the right side of the cardstock, covering all of the white.
- Use the Distressing Tip to distress the edges of the leaf embellishments. Layer them on top of each other and adhere.

- Distress an 11-inch section of the white paper ribbon. Adhere it across both pages as shown.
- Punch 8 tags from the White Shimmer Cardstock using the Tag Maker and distress them. Adhere them so they are positioned against the ribbon.
- Print or handwrite the journaling question on a strip of White Shimmer Cardstock. Tear the ends and adhere over the ribbon.

Continued

Ted & Emily should
a**ways**

Spread 5

5th two-page spread

- Trim green patterned paper to 12" x 8." Then cut 4 inches off one edge.
- Adhere the 4-inch piece to the left side of an 8" x 8" piece of White Cardstock.
- Crop photo to 5" x 8." Adhere as shown.
- Print or handwrite "Ted & Emily should" on White Shimmer Cardstock. Cut a half circle using the inside of the large Circle Pattern and the red blade. Adhere to the page over a blue tag. Add the word "always" with stickers.
- Cut 3 White Shimmer Cardstock circles with the outside of the small Circle Pattern and the green blade. Adhere across the bottom of the green papers.
- Trim $3\frac{1}{2}$" x 8" strips. Place them across the bottoms of the pages and along the edge of the photo.
- Punch 3 blue hearts and adhere over the circles.

What do you think is in store for Ted & Emily?

Spread 6

MILESTONE GIFTS

6th two-page spread

- Trim 2 sheets of White Shimmer Cardstock to 8″ x 8.″
- Punch 10 green and 11 blue puzzle pieces. Line them up as shown, using some to make a frame.
- Trim the photo to 4″ x 5½″ and round the corners using the Corner Maker. Adhere over the puzzle frame.
- Print or handwrite the journaling on White Shimmer Cardstock. Trim and adhere below the puzzle pieces.
- Trim a green tag and adhere on the top of the page.

Tips

- *This is a project that might require help gathering photos of the couple. Find out if they had engagement photos taken.*
- *Remember to bring enough pens for people to use.*
- *Bring the album and pages with you to the event so you can slip away and put it all together to give to the couple. They'll love it!*

Continued

How many children do you think Ted & Emily will have?

Spread 7

7th two-page spread

- Trim a sheet of White Shimmer Cardstock to 8" x 8." Repeat with the green patterned paper.
- Print or handwrite the question on an 8" x 1½" strip of green patterned paper. Adhere to the bottom of the White Shimmer Cardstock.
- Cut a gray circle using the inside of the largest Circle Pattern and the red and blue blades. Adhere to the center of the White Shimmer Cardstock. Place a black question mark sticker in the center. Punch a blue heart and adhere. Embellish with a paper flower.

- Crop the photo to 5½" x 7" and round the corners. Adhere.
- Embellish with the "dreams" sticker. Add the leaf tag. Punch another blue heart and adhere it with a flower.
- Crop photo to 5½" x 8" and adhere to the right side of the spread.

Ted,
you should
ALWAYS...

Spread 8

8th two-page spread

- Trim 2 sheets of White Shimmer Cardstock to 8″ x 8.″
- Trim two 8″ x 1″ pieces of green patterned paper and adhere to the bottom of the White Shimmer Cardstock.
- Trim a piece of 1½″ x 2″ gray paper. Adhere to the bottom-right side of the layout. Print or handwrite the question on White Cardstock, trim and adhere over the gray.

- Cut triangles from the green patterned paper. Hand cut a thin, curved strip of the gray paper. Flip it over, and use Precision Point Adhesive to hold the triangles evenly along the back edge. Adhere the pennant to the layout.
- Crop the photo to 5½″ x 7″ and position as shown.

Continued

Spread 9

9th two-page spread

- Trim 2 sheets of White Shimmer Cardstock to 8″ x 8.″
- Use the Border Maker to punch a picket fence border from blue paper. Adhere to the top of both sheets. Repeat for the bottom.
- Crop the photo to 5″ x 8″ and adhere.
- Print or handwrite the journaling on White Shimmer Cardstock. Punch a heart out of the blue patterned paper and trim about ³⁄₄ of an inch around the empty space. Place the heart opening over the journaling on the White Shimmer Cardstock and adhere. Trim the cardstock.

- Place your heart/frame on the green patterned paper, with the right side of the paper facing down. Tear the green paper with the Scallop Tearing Tool, trying to keep the distance uniform. Leave about a ¹⁄₂ inch around the blue frame. Fold the green scallops over the blue frame, so the pattern is right-side up. Trim the corners as needed and adhere. Use the Corner Maker to round them.
- Adhere the heart/frame embellishment in the corner as shown.

Spread 10

10th two-page spread

- Trim 2 sheets of White Shimmer Cardstock pages to 8″ x 8.″
- Trim the blue patterned paper to 12″ x 8.″ Hand cut some curves with your scissors. You will use the top, bottom and middle blue pieces. Adhere these across the 16″ x 8″ spread as shown, being careful to adhere the edges well.
- Crop the photo to 4½″ x 8″ and adhere as shown.
- Print or handwrite the question on White Shimmer Cardstock and trim to the inside of the medium Circle Pattern with the green blade. Trim the gray patterned paper using the same pattern with the red blade. Layer these circles and position them as shown. Place a 1″ x 8″ gray patterned paper border along the edge, overlapping the photo and the edge of the circles.
- Punch 3 small white circles and two small gray circles with the Circle Maker. Evenly adhere them along the left side of the spread as shown.
- Cut 3 gray circles using the inside of the smallest Circle Pattern and the red and green blades. Adhere.
- Punch 3 blue hearts with the Sweet Heart Maker and adhere. Punch 2 hearts with the Lovable Mini Pocket Punch out of White Shimmer Cardstock and adhere. Add a blue heart on the question circle.

Continued

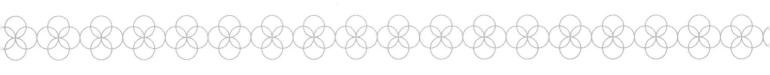

> What is your wish
> for Ted & Emily?

Spread 11

11th two-page spread

- Trim 2 sheets of White Shimmer Cardstock to 8" x 8."
- Use the Border Maker to punch three 12-inch frame chain borders out of blue patterned paper. Position them so they overlap, as shown, and adhere. Cover the corners with small white flowers.
- Crop the photo to $4^3/_4$" x 8" and adhere as shown.
- Adhere the blue scalloped tag.
- Print or handwrite the journaling on White Shimmer Cardstock. Trim and adhere over the scalloped tag.

Closing page

- Trim a sheet of White Shimmer Cardstock to 8" x 8."
- Print or handwrite your text at the top of the page.
- Trim blue paper to 8" x 4" and adhere.
- Crop photo to $2^3/_4$" x $3^3/_4$" and round the corners. Adhere.
- Cut the gray tag in half. Adhere (slide the edges under each side of the photo).

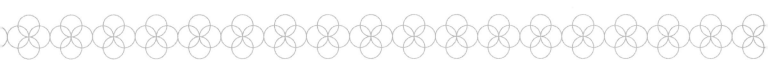

"From every human being there rises a light that reaches straight to heaven. And when two souls that are destined to be together find each other, their streams of light flow together, and a single brighter light goes forth from their united being."

Author Unknown

Closing Page

RECIPES FOR...

Album pages for an 8 x 8 Recipe Quick Album

Making my Mom's biscuits together with Ashby brings back so many memories of making them with my Mom. Ashby loves to make them and even more, eat them. I love knowing that this favorite family recipe of Mom's will be passed on.

One of my favorite products on which I've worked with Creative Memories is my Recipe Quick Album. And one of the things I love most about it is having family members record their recipes in their own handwriting – like I did here with my mom's specialty: Betty's Biscuits. Favorite dishes are among the most special of family traditions and would make an amazing gift for everyone in the family. Or what about a book filled with healthy recipes to help you teach kids the importance of good nutrition? But you don't have to stick with a literal approach for the Recipe Quick Album. Think about giving your recipes for success to a young graduate or your recipes for a happy marriage to a new couple. Try some of the ideas you'll find on these next few pages.

Recipes for... Betty's Biscuits

Ingredients:

8 x 8 Recipe Quick Album

Tape Runner

Instructions:

- For the left side of the layout, use the white paper with brown flower accents and the horizontal yellow photo mat as the base.
- Adhere a 6″ x 4″ recipe card to the yellow photo mat.
- Add the cherry tag die-cut shape to the right of the recipe. Add a 2″ x 2″ photo.
- For the right side of the layout, use the yellow paper with red stripes as the base.
- Adhere a 4″ x 6″ photo.
- Adhere the "Sugar & Spice" title sticker to the rolling pin die-cut shape. Adhere to the layout. Add the canisters die-cut shape. Add journaling as desired.

Continued

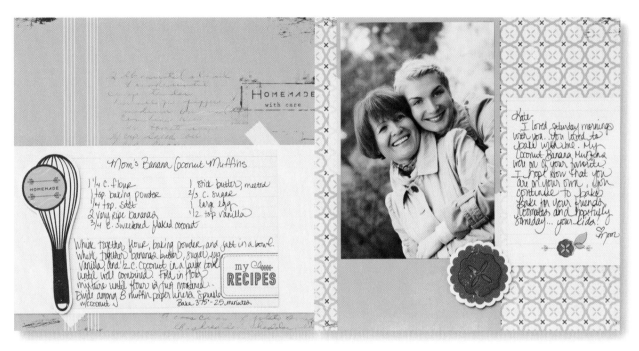

Recipes for... Graduation/College

Ingredients:

8 x 8 Recipe Quick Album
Brown Dual-Tip Pen
Tape Runner

Instructions:

• Use the green paper with the white bar across the bottom as the base for the left side of the spread.

• Add the horizontal recipe card with the red "my recipes" in the bottom-right corner and the Brown Dual-Tip Pen to write your recipe.

• Add the beater die-cut shape to the left side of the layout.

• Use the green pie-patterned paper with the green bar along the left side as the base for the right side of the spread.

• Adhere a 4" x 6" photo to the green bar.

• Add the red pie die-cut shape.

• Journal using the Brown Dual-Tip Pen.

Recipes for...
A new bride

Ingredients:

8 x 8 Recipe Quick Album

Brown Dual-Tip Pen

Tape Runner

Instructions:

• Use the yellow patterned paper with the white photo mat as the base for the left side of the spread.

• Adhere a 6″ x 4″ photo to the white photo mat.

• Add the blue pie die-cut shape.

• Use the blue patterned paper with the blue photo mat as the base for the right side of the spread.

• Adhere a horizontal recipe card with the blue outline to the top right of the layout, flush with the right side.

• Adhere a vertical recipe card with the brown outline to the blue photo mat, overlapping the horizontal recipe card.

• Add the "Savor the Memories" title sticker to the recipe card.

• Journal using the Brown Dual-Tip Pen.

Continued

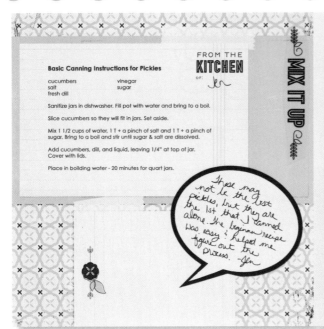

Recipes for...
Family favorites

Ingredients:

8 x 8 Recipe Quick Album

Black Cardstock

White Shimmer Cardstock

All-Purpose Scissors

Corner Maker

12-inch Rotary Trimmer

Custom Cutting System
   (with Oval Patterns)

Tape Runner

Font: Century Gothic

Instructions for each spread:

- Trim a sheet of White Shimmer Cardstock to 8″ x 8.″ Print and crop a photo to 7″ x 7″ and round the corners. Mat with Black Cardstock and round the mat corners. Adhere.
- Choose a sheet of patterned paper. Print the recipe on a recipe mat and adhere.
- Create the thought bubble by using the inside of the larger Oval Pattern and the green blade to cut most of an oval from the recipe mat papers. Don't cut all of the way around the oval – leave about a quarter inch attached.
- Use scissors to trim the attached part into a point.
- Repeat with Black Cardstock and the red blade. Use the scissors to make a similar point with the Black Cardstock.
- Have a family member journal on the thought bubble – it can be anything to do with the food.

Phyllis's Granola Bars

2 cups old fashioned oats
1/3 cup shredded coconut
1 cup sliced almonds

2 TBSP butter
1/2 cup honey
1/4 cup brown sugar

2 TBSP ground flax seed
1/3 cup chocolate chips

Toast the almonds, oatmeal, and coconut at 350 degrees for 10 minutes.

Combine honey, butter, and brown sugar in sauce pan. Heat over medium until brown sugar dissolves.

Combine toasted ingredients with wet ingredients. Add chocolate chips and flax seed, then pat into 8x8 pan.

Bake at 300 degrees for 20 minutes.

Let cool and slice.

"Yum. Can I have another one?"

— Noah

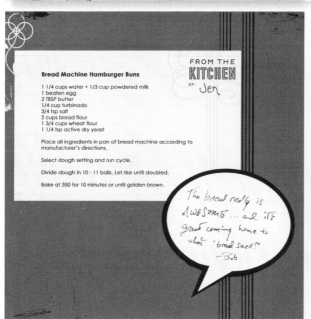

Bread Machine Hamburger Buns

1 1/4 cups water + 1/3 cup powdered milk
1 beaten egg
2 TBSP butter
1/4 cup turbinado
3/4 tsp salt
2 cups bread flour
1 3/4 cups wheat flour
1 1/4 tsp active dry yeast

Place all ingredients in pan of bread machine according to manufacturer's directions.

Select dough setting and run cycle.

Divide dough in 10 - 11 balls. Let rise until doubled.

Bake at 350 for 10 minutes or until golden brown.

FROM THE **KITCHEN** OF: *Jen*

The bread really is AWESOME ... and it's great coming home to that "bread smell!"

—Bob

Continued

OTHER RECIPE ALBUM OPTIONS

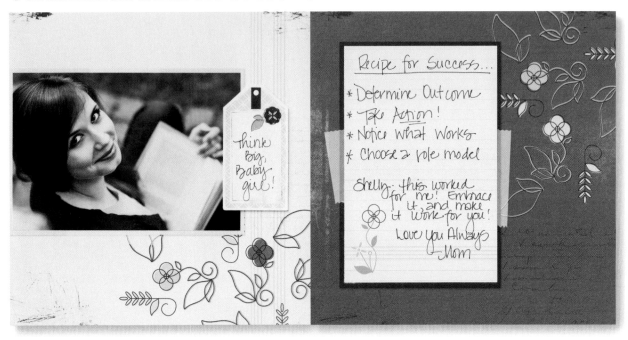

Think Big, Baby girl!

Recipe for Success...
* Determine Outcome
* Take Action!
* Notice what Works
* Choose a role model

Shelly, this worked for me! Embrace it, and make it work for you! Love you Always —Mom

Recipes for...
Success

Ingredients:

8 x 8 Recipe Quick Album
Brown Dual-Tip Pen
Tape Runner

Instructions:

- Use the cream paper with the flower accent and the horizontal yellow photo mat as the base for the left side of the spread.
- Adhere a 6" x 4" photo to the yellow photo mat.
- Add the yellow tag die-cut shape to the right of the photo and the Brown Dual-Tip Pen to journal.
- Use the red paper with the flower accents and the vertical brown photo mat as the base for the right side of the spread.
- Use the vertical recipe card with the green lines at the bottom and the Brown Dual-Tip Pen to write your recipe.

Recipes for...
A happy marriage

Ingredients:

8 x 8 Recipe Quick Album

Brown Dual-Tip Pen

Tape Runner

Instructions:

- Use the red patterned paper with the teal photo mat as the base for the left side of the spread.
- Adhere a 4" x 6" photo to the teal photo mat.
- Add the "Made With Love" clear title sticker to the top of the photo.
- Use the cream patterned paper with the green photo mat as the base for the right side of the spread.
- Use the vertical recipe card with the red lines at the bottom and the Brown Dual-Tip Pen to write your recipe. Use the clear title stickers to add to the recipe.
- Add the tag die-cut shape to the bottom corner of the recipe card. Add the pear die-cut to the tag. Journal using the Brown Dual-Tip Pen.

Continued

ADVICE FOR NEW PARENTS

Album pages for a 4 x 6 PicFolio® Album

Now, I'm not going to say there are no good pregnancy or baby books out there. ("Full of Life: Mom-to-Mom Tips I Wish Someone Had Told Me When I Was Pregnant" comes to mind...) But if you have specific advice of your own to give to someone special, we have some simple ideas for putting it together.

A 4 x 6 PicFolio® Photo Album is perfect for a project like this. Twenty-four slip-in sleeves – enough to have some substance, but not so much that it can't be read in the space of the average nap! Think about making this album ahead of time and bringing it to a baby shower. (Maybe leave a few blank pages at the end for guests to contribute their own advice!)

Ingredients:

4 x 6 PicFolio® Photo Album

Fabulous Power® Palette (for girl)

Rugged Power® Palette (for boy)

Personal Trimmer

12-inch Rotary Trimmer

Tape Runner

Instructions:

• Use photo mats and a few embellishments for this project.

• Print or handwrite your advice "headline" on photo mat paper, adding stars above and below. Adhere paper ribbon or a ½-inch paper strip to embellish.

• Print or handwrite detailed advice on a coordinating photo mat and embellish at the bottom.

• Intersperse advice pages with photos of the couple, pregnant mother, baby or friends. Adhere photos to photo mats and add paper ribbons, flowers or buttons as desired.

★★★★★★★★★★★★★★★★★★★★★★★★

Always Sleep When The Baby Is Sleeping

★★★★★★★★★★★★★★★★★★★★★★★★

Everyone tells you this as a soon-to-be mother, and you think "yes, I know, I know!" It doesn't become completely real until you get up in the morning and can count in minutes how much sleep you have had the night before. Combine that with all you feel like you *have* to do and you may end up doing chores during those precious nap times. Remember this: the chores will still be there when you wake up, but your well being may not! It is important to rejuvenate and get those needed zzzz's during the day so you are ready to tackle those sleepless nights and busy days.

Continued

Don't Compare Your Baby With Other Babies

It is so easy to get sucked into the trap of comparing what your baby does to babies of other ages and to what other mothers say their babies have done. You start to worry why your baby isn't sleeping, crawling, sitting up, cooing, eating, walking, solving equations, etc. All babies are different. Period. What one baby does is completely different from what other babies will do. There are even differences within families on when and how babies meet milestones. You may have expectations with a subsequent birth, but it's likely that baby will do things on his/her own schedule!

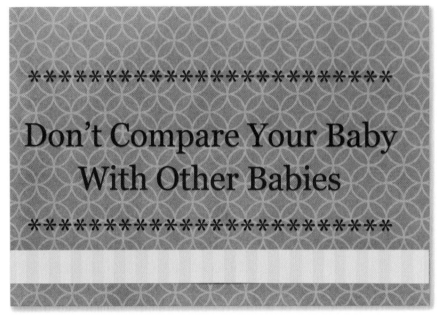

****

Accept Help From Others

****

Up until this point you've probably been a fairly independent person that can do most things for yourself, especially those mundane daily chores you do without thinking about it. This all turns upside down after a baby comes into your life. Just showering is an extreme chore some days. It's perfectly ok to accept help from family, friends and neighbors when they offer it. They're going to the store? Sure, let them pick up some milk. They bring you dinner or offer dinner? Hey, it's one less chore you need to worry about that day and you can take care of yourself and your baby. Helping is valuable!

Continued

The Books Don't Have All The Baby Answers

The baby books, oh the wonderfully informative baby books! You might read and re-read these books about what you can expect as a new parent and what your baby may or may not do. What ends up happening many times is that your baby isn't doing these things, or your baby is doing 5 at once and you have absolutely no idea what will come next or what you should be doing. My advice? Throw the books out for a while and just focus on listening to your baby and yourself. Babies never fit neatly into the categories books put them into and they shouldn't. Your baby has his/her own personality and way of doing things that you will learn through the weeks and months that they come into your life!

****

Take Time For You

****

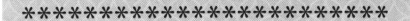

MOM

It is so important to take some time for yourself after the baby comes. You will feel like all you do throughout the day should be for your new bundle and your needs and wants will take a back seat for months and years to come. It is very important to continue to do things for yourself, which can be as small as a nice long shower or as big as a shopping excursion for an afternoon or day. Moms are allowed to take care of themselves and feel good about themselves, while at the same time taking care of their little ones. It's important and also necessary to feel good!

LOVE IS...

12 x 12 page for a Magnetic Everyday Display

When you're sure it's love, you want to tell the world. Here's a fun little tribute to love with some rich pops of red and a few great photos. Make one for a daughter and her new fiancé. Make one for a dear friend who's found someone special. Or make one for yourself and your sweetheart. It might go up on Valentine's Day, but it looks so good and the sentiment is so timeless, this could stay on your wall for a while.

Ingredients:

Sleek Black Magnetic Everyday Display

Black & White Designer-Print Paper

Black & White Tone-on-Tone Paper

Black & White Storybox

Black Cardstock

Cranberry Cardstock

White Cardstock

Black Simple ABC/123 Stickers

Corner Maker

Sweet Heart Maker

Border Maker System (with Scallop Stitch Cartridge)

All-Purpose Scissors

12-inch Rotary Trimmer

Precision Point Adhesive

Foam Squares

Tape Runner

Font: Vladimir Script

Instructions:

- Cut graph-ruled paper to 8½" x 7¼." Adhere to upper-left side of a sheet of Cranberry Cardstock.

- Cut floral paper to 3¼" x 7¼." Adhere to upper-right side of background.

- Use the Border Maker and Scallop Stitch Cartridge to punch three scallop border strips from polka dot paper (1½" x 7¼", 1¼" x 7¼" and 1" x 7¼"). Layer strips together, largest at the bottom, and adhere to left side of floral paper. Hide seams using White Cardstock cut to ½" x 7¼."

- Adhere 7" x 5" photo to graph-ruled paper on the left, 1½ inches from top edge of page. Affix title above photo using ABC Stickers.

- Cut a 12" x 1½" strip of Cranberry Cardstock. Adhere to hide seams of patterned papers above. Add a 1" x 12" strip of Black Cardstock through the center.

- Use the Sweet Heart Maker to punch 5 hearts from Cranberry Cardstock. Adhere 2 of the large hearts above photo (one tucked behind photo and one atop photo) using Precision Point Adhesive. Adhere the last 3 large hearts below the Black Cardstock strip in a random row.

- Adhere the smaller hearts to each large heart using Foam Squares.

- Print or handwrite love quote on White Cardstock. Using Corner Maker, round corners on left side. Adhere toward bottom of page to the right side of hearts.

- Adhere two 2" x 3" photos to 2¼" x 3¼" pieces of White Cardstock and adhere to right side of love quote, layered together and angled.

BIRTHDAY WISHES

Album pages for a 12 x 12 scrapbook album

HAPPY bIRTHday

Wishes for Riely (6) and Owen (7)

"Annual update" albums have been around for a while. But there's no height, weight or favorite foods here. This one captures wishes. Each year, include a photo of the child blowing out candles. The facing page can record his or her wishes, party guests' wishes or your wishes for your children as they grow over the next year. Watch the way those wishes change over the years. Then send the album, and all those wishes, along when they move out on their own.

Ingredients:

12 x 12 Coverset

12 x 12 White Scrapbook Pages

Fabulous Power® Palette

Taffy Cardstock

White Cardstock

White Ruled Paper

Corner Maker

12-inch Rotary Trimmer

Foam Squares

Tape Runner

Instructions:

- Adhere 2 sheets of White Ruled Paper onto teal patterned papers. Add paper ribbon to top and bottom edges.
- Place a 5″ x 7″ photo on left page. Use Decorative ABC Stickers to spell out title. Print or handwrite journaling on Taffy Cardstock, trim and adhere. Add paper flowers and buttons.
- Mat a title sticker on White Cardstock, round the corners and mount it with Foam Squares on a slightly larger rectangle cut from a photo mat. Round those corners as well. Adhere it in the top corner of right page with more flowers and buttons.

GRANDPARENTS' BRAG BOOK

Album pages for an 8 x 8 scrapbook album

Photos and updates are like oxygen for grandparents – especially if they live out of town. So don't forget to share! Here are some simple-but-beautiful layout ideas to help you put together a little 8 x 8 brag book album. Grandma and Grandpa are going to be showing off the photos you send them anyway. Make it something that shows and tells just how special that new grandbaby is!

No matter what hat he wears, he still looks adorable!

it's a BOY

Ingredients:

8 x 8 Coverset

8 x 8 Scrapbook Pages

8 x 8 Scrapbook Kit (Rugged Baby
    Boy OR Fabulous Baby Girl)

White Cardstock

White Simple Monogram Stickers

12-inch Rotary Trimmer

Border Maker System (with Picket
    Fence Cartridge for boy OR
    Scallop Stitch Cartridge for girl)

Custom Cutting System
    (with Circle Patterns)

Foam Squares

Tape Runner

Instructions:

It's a Boy/It's a Girl

• Trim a piece of green paper to 8″ x 4″ and adhere to background paper. Cover seam with an 8″ x 2½″ strip of yellow
  paper for boy, pink paper for girl. Adhere four 2″ x 2″ photos across middle strip.

• Trim stars for boy or flowers for girl from patterned paper and adhere them to lower-left side with Foam Squares.

• Apply a title sticker to cardstock and trim it. Adhere with Foam Squares.

• Print or handwrite journaling on White Cardstock. Cut into strips and adhere to page.

Continued

Love those

beautiful gray eyes!

4 months old

cuddle time with froggy
makes sam smile!

Page 2

- Trim a piece of patterned paper to 8″ x 4″ and adhere to one side of background page.
- Use the Border Maker (Picket Fence for boy, Scallop Stitch for girl) to punch a border using complementing paper. Adhere it to your page, just right of center.
- Place 3 photos vertically along edge of punched border.
- Apply stickers to cardstock and trim them; adhere with Foam Squares to the bottom-left corner.
- Print or handwrite journaling on White Cardstock. Cut into strips and adhere to page.

Continued

Page 3

• Select a piece of patterned paper for a background (blue for boy, purple for girl). Trim a coordinating sheet (yellow for boy, white for girl) to 8″ x 5½″, cut holes with the Circle Patterns as shown and adhere to the right edge of your background.

• Mat photo on photo mat and adhere to center of page.

• Apply title sticker to cardstock and trim it. Adhere with Foam Squares .

• Print or handwrite journaling on White Cardstock. Cut into strips and adhere to page.

Page 4

- Use Custom Cutting System Circles to cut pieces from patterned paper (text for boy, patterned stripe for girl).
  Adhere circles all over background paper (gray for boy, pink for girl) with Foam Squares. Trim off any overhang.
- Adhere photo to photo mat, then adhere to center of page.
- Stick a monogram sticker in lower-left corner of photo.
- Apply stickers to cardstock and trim them. Adhere with Foam Squares.
- Print or handwrite journaling on White Cardstock. Cut into strips and adhere to page.

LOVE AT FIRST SIGHT

12 x 12 page for a Magnetic Everyday Display

Here's a beautiful take on a newborn gift that's flexible enough to grow with the child. It's a cute-but-clean context for some beautiful baby photos. And the questionnaire lets you fill in all the delightful details. This is classic baby stuff. But since it's mounted on a Magnetic Everyday Display, those new parents will have a little celebration station to update, decorate and grow with their child for years. (Use Rugged Baby Boy Arrival Additions to alter this recipe for a boy!)

Ingredients:

Weathered Black Magnetic Everyday Display

Fabulous Baby Girl Arrival Additions

Taffy Cardstock

Blossom Place 'n' Punch

All-Purpose Scissors

12-inch Rotary Trimmer

Border Maker System (with Scallop Stitch Cartridge)

Custom Cutting System (with Circle Patterns)

Precision Point Adhesive

Foam Squares

Tape Runner

Instructions:

• Cut the birth announcement from the Fabulous Baby Girl Arrival Additions to 11″ x 4¼.″

• Cut Taffy Cardstock to 11¼″ x 4¾.″ Adhere trimmed birth announcement.

• Using the Custom Cutting System, cut a circle from the purple floral photo mat. Adhere stork sticker. Using Blossom Place 'n' Punch, punch 5 flowers from the printed paper. Adhere 2 of them to the right of the stork using Foam Squares, then adhere your circle to the birth announcement.

• Using the Border Maker, punch 3 scallop borders from the teal paper. Trim each border to 1¼ inches. Layer the scalloped borders on top of each other and adhere to the top of a sheet of floral-patterned paper with the yellow stripe.

• Adhere a 6″ x 4″ photo to a pink floral photo mat and adhere to the page. Adhere 3″ x 4½″ and 2″ x 3″ photos to right of large photo.

• Adhere title sticker and embellish with hearts.

• Use Foam Squares to adhere 3 remaining cut flowers to the top-left corner of page. Adhere title sticker next to flowers and above photo.

GRADUATION WISHES

Digital layout for a 30 x 20 poster

MY LIFE, RIGHT NOW

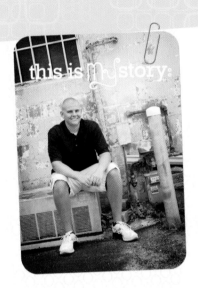
this is my story:

WHAT ADVICE DO YOU HAVE FOR JOSH AS HE STARTS THE NEXT CHAPTER OF HIS LIFE? SIGN YOUR NAME & LEAVE HIM A FEW WORDS.

Actually this simple poster project is a lot like all those grads out there: So much potential! We've included a photo and an invitation to leave some advice – along with plenty of room to write. If you're planning an open house for your graduate, this is a great addition to a table full of photos and albums. And when it's finished, your grad gets a simple source of inspiration from his guests that will fit on the wall of any apartment or dorm!

Ingredients:

StoryBook Creator 4.0 Software

Reflections Digital Power® Palette

Office Supplies Silver Digital Embellishments

Font: Base '02

Instructions:

• Open a blank 30″ x 20″ Wall Print. Fill the background with a patterned paper that coordinates with your photo. (Under the Color Ribbon, adjust the hue in the paper if necessary.)

• Insert a folder from the Geometric Shapes Content Library. Fill the file folder with a light-colored paper and adjust the color so it is light enough for guests to write on.

• Insert a text box, type "2012" and make it fit in the tab of the folder. Reduce the opacity to 15 percent.

• Insert the "My Life, Right Now" embellishment. Recolor it black. Position it over the "2012" you just added.

• Insert the photo. Rotate it slightly. Insert the partial paper clip from the Office Supplies Kit and position it so that it appears to hold the photo to the folder.

• Insert the "This Is My Story" embellishment. Position it on the photo as shown and recolor it white.

• Add another text box. Use a dark gray font color and type the instructions to the guests. Position at the bottom of the folder.

• Group all of the elements except the background paper. Rotate them as one unit (so it stays aligned).

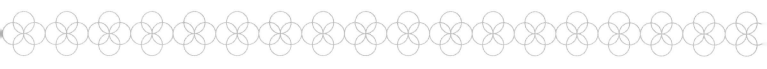

WELCOME TO OUR HOME

Digital layout for a Photo Panel

The Lessingers

welcome
to our home.

est. 2008

Here's a housewarming gift that will really bring down the house! A Digital Photo Panel like this is easy, unique and practical. It's a snap to create in Creative Memories StoryBook Creator 4.0 Software and can be designed to match any décor. A simple Photo Panel similar to this would also be a great gift for teachers or newlyweds!

Ingredients:

StoryBook Creator 4.0 Software

Fabulous Digital Power® Palette

Font: HandTIMES

Instructions:

- Open a 12″ x 12″ blank Photo Panel project. Choose a photo and size it so it covers the width of the panel.
- Insert 2 pink ribbons, one blue and one yellow, from the Fabulous Digital Power Palette. Place the wider pink ribbons at the bottom of the photo and the bottom of the page. If desired, use the Color Ribbon to change the color of the ribbon to match something in your photo.
- Position the yellow ribbon just above the bottom orange ribbon. Place the final ribbon on top of the yellow ribbon. Again, recolor to match photo, if desired.

- Insert a text box and type "Welcome" at 96 pt. Make the text white.
- Insert another text box. Type "to our home" at 48 pt. Again, make the text white.
- Insert a third text box and type your last name. Use 32 pt. font.
- Insert a fourth text box and type "est. (year married)." Use 28 pt. font.

HAPPY BIRTHDAY

12 x 12 page for a Magnetic Everyday Display

*When you're a kid, it's tough to pick the **best** thing about birthdays. But, clearly, the **worst** thing for a kid is that they only last one day. Hang this in your birthday child's room for a few weeks to help relive the good times and remind him how special he is. (It's on a Magnetic Everyday Display, so it's easy to update and move on to the next milestone!)*

Ingredients:

Sleek White Magnetic Everyday Display

Cheerful Birthday Additions

Cheerful Paper Ribbon

Royal Blue Cardstock

White Cardstock

White Simple Monogram Stickers

Border Maker System (with Picket Fence Cartridge)

Circle Maker

All-Purpose Scissors

12-inch Rotary Trimmer

Precision Point Adhesive

Foam Squares

Tape Runner

Font: Calibri

Instructions:

- Use the Border Maker to punch a $1\frac{1}{2}''$ x 12″ picket fence border of a Cheerful Birthday Paper and set aside the 6 zigzag scraps. Thread the border with blue paper ribbon and adhere it to the bottom of a Royal Blue Cardstock background.

- Trim a $\frac{1}{2}''$ x 12″ strip of a Cheerful Birthday Paper. (We've cut ours to be just the green cupcakes.) Adhere it to the top of the page.

- Adhere the zigzag scraps from the first step along the top of the page against your green cupcake strip.

- Affix a title sticker to the upper-left corner.

- Use the Circle Maker to punch three $1\frac{1}{2}$-inch circles from photo mats. Fold each in half.

- Trim two 17-inch strips of polka dot paper ribbon.

- Adhere the folded circles to the ribbon strips, fold a loop at each ribbon's end and position as shown.

- Print or handwrite journaling on the left side of a green photo mat, trim to $4\frac{1}{2}''$ x $5\frac{1}{2}''$ and adhere as shown.

- Punch a $1\frac{3}{4}''$ x $5\frac{1}{2}''$ border strip, thread with striped paper ribbon and adhere to right side of journaling mat. Add a sticker using Foam Squares.

- Mat a 4″ x 6″ photo on a $4\frac{1}{4}''$ x $6\frac{1}{4}''$ rectangle of White Cardstock and adhere it to the left of the journaling. Add a sticker, using Foam Squares.

- Hand cut a small and medium-sized blue cupcake from a Cheerful Birthday Paper and adhere small cupcake to medium cupcake using Foam Squares.

- Adhere White Simple Monogram Sticker number, using Foam Squares, and embellish with a sticker. Place the embellished cupcake as shown.

HAPPY ANNIVERSARY!

12 x 12 Page Print for a Page Frame

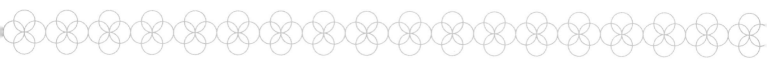

Celebrating 60 (or 50, or 40...you get the idea) years of marriage is a treasured event. For celebrations like this, create something big and bold to spotlight the love of the anniversary couple. Before you put the digital page print inside the Page Frame, let the guests at the party write messages of congratulations all around the print on the frame's mat.

Ingredients:

StoryBook Creator 4.0 Software

Gratitude Series Digital Kit

Font: Levinim MT & Dear Sarah Rg

Instructions:

- Add Paper 04 to the left side of your project. Add Paper 15 to the right side leaving white space between the papers.
- Add Paper 07. Cut into a circle. Add a heavy shadow.
- Add the Blue Ribbon, Blue Word Border and Orange Ribbon embellishments. Add a heavy shadow to the Blue Word Border.
- Add a 4" x 6" photo and a 2.5" x 3.5" photo. Add a heavy shadow to each. Angle as shown. Add two Photo Corners to each photo.
- Add the Love embellishment.

- Add the "If you have lived" title in the upper-right corner. Add a light shadow.
- Add the "Thanksgiving after all" title. Under the Cut & Fill tab, create a rectangle to delete the wording, leaving only the swirls and flowers. Enlarge and arrange behind the photos as shown.
- Add years and names as desired.
- Upload to creativememories.com to place your order.
- Put digital print into Page Frame.

Holiday Gifts

It's no surprise that holidays have the potential to bring as much stress as they do joy. Time gets short. Budgets get tight. And so many of us feel pressure to find "the perfect gift" or to nail it for that person "who has everything." Yikes!

We've packed this chapter with ideas for gifts, decorations and keepsakes. Some are quick and simple, while others are more involved. But each idea is built around the photos, stories and sentiments of the season.

If you've ever wondered how to make Thanksgiving about more than turkey, cranberries and football, we can help. Or if you'd like your Christmas to be more about peace and joy than your niece's new toys, you're in the right place.

Chapter 3 Recipes

TEN FAVORITE MEMORIES OF DAD

Album pages for a 4 x 6 PicFolio® Album

*If your dad is anything like mine, then shopping is a challenge. Sure, he'll be perfectly happy on Father's Day with your gift of ties and cologne – but will **you**? Here's a great idea for giving Dad something he can't help but love. These 4 x 6 PicFolio® Photo Albums are amazingly quick and easy. (The cover even comes with a strap to flip it over and display it like an easel, so Dad can keep it out on the end table, right next to his favorite chair.)*

Ingredients:

4 x 6 PicFolio® Photo Album

Rugged Storybox Photo Mats

Rugged Title Stickers

Rugged Paper Frames

Rugged Paper Ribbon

Rugged Paper Tags

White Cardstock

12-inch Rotary Trimmer

Foam Squares

Tape Runner

Instructions:

• Create a title page by layering paper ribbon, tags and stickers with Foam Squares. Adhere to red photo mat. Add stickers to White Cardstock, trim out and adhere below title.

• For each page, apply paper ribbon to background photo mats. Adhere 1 photo per page.

• Print or handwrite journaling on White Cardstock and coordinating patterned paper. Cut into strips and apply to each page.

Continued

MEMORY Nº. 3

MEMORY Nº. 4

Family Photos with
lots of corduroy & gigantic
shirt collars

The Peterson Family   circa 1977

MEMORY Nº. 6

MEMORY Nº. 5

Expeditions into the woods
to cut firewood &
gather kindling

Daddy, Josh, Lisa & Grandpa Peterson   OCT. 1976

MEMORY Nº. 7

The roar of Dad's Harley

during the Fourth of July

parade in Granby

Dad on his HD Road King JULY 2006

MEMORY Nº. 8

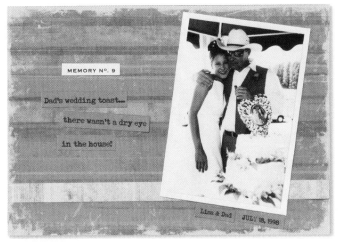

MEMORY Nº. 9

Dad's wedding toast...

there wasn't a dry eye

in the house!

Lisa & Dad   JULY 18, 1998

MEMORY Nº. 10

Making Dad a Grandpa

with the birth

of Hayden Grey

Nana, Grandpa & Uncle Josh (with Baby Hayden)

JAN. 2001

YOU & ME

Album pages for a 12 x 12 scrapbook album

I love you not because of who you are,
but because of who I am when I am with you.

july 2011

YOU & ME

You say your love keeps growing? Why not start growing a valentine to match! Each year, instead of a card on Valentine's Day, add a special page or two to your You & Me album. As time goes by, you'll build a gigantic, unique, very special album. And every February, it will get even more beautiful.

Ingredients:

12 x 12 Coverset

12 x 12 White Scrapbook Pages

Reflections Designer-Print Paper

Reflections Title Stickers

Reflections Decorative ABC Stickers

Reflections Paper Flowers

Reflections Paper Ribbon

Reflections Paper Tags

White Cardstock

White Shimmer Cardstock

Black and Gray Dual-Tip Pens

Lovable Mini Pocket Punches

Postage Stamp Place 'n' Punch

12-inch Rotary Trimmer

Border Maker System (with Scallop Stitch and Frame Chain Cartridges)

Custom Cutting System (with Circle Patterns)

Foam Squares

Tape Runner

Instructions:

Page 1

- Trim large heart from light-blue pattern paper and adhere to White Shimmer Cardstock.
- Use the Border Maker to punch scallops from gray paper and adhere around edge of heart.
- Apply photo strip with Foam Squares.
- Trim flower from patterned paper and cluster together with paper tags and leaves in lower-right corner. Apply title sticker.
- Trim small flower from light-blue patterned paper and adhere to heart using Foam Square.
- Print or handwrite journaling on White Cardstock. Cut into strips and adhere to page.

Page 2

- Print or handwrite journaling on gray patterned paper.
- Punch frame chain border from White Cardstock using the Border Maker. Adhere across top of page, then adhere photo to top edge.
- Add paper tags, ribbon and flowers to top and bottom edges.
- Punch a postage stamp from gray paper and write name and date with black pen. Adhere to lower left. Use ABC sticker as flower center.

Continued

She keeps it simple
and I am thankful for her kind of lovin'
'Cause it's simple

No longer do we wonder
if we're together, we're way past that
And I've already asked her
So in January we're gettin' married

She's talkin' to me with her voice
down so low I barely hear her
But I know what she's sayin'
I understand because my heart
and hers are the same
And in January we're gettin' married

And I was sick with heartache
And she was sick like Audrey Hepburn when I met her
But we would both surrender
True love is not the kind of thing you should turn down
Don't ever turn it down

I hope that I don't sound too insane when I say
There is darkness all around us
I don't feel weak but I do need sometimes
for her to protect me
and reconnect me to the beauty that I'm missin'
And in January we're gettin' married

No longer does it matter what circumstances we were born in
She knows which birds are singin'
and the names of the trees
where they're performing in the mornin'
And in January we're gettin' married

lisa & mike
APR. 1998

Page 2

Page 3

- Print or handwrite journaling on blue patterned paper.
- Adhere 4″ x 6″ photo to center of page, just right of the journaling.
- Trim piece of patterned paper to 4″ x 6.″ Adhere to the right of photo.
- Add a strip of paper ribbon across the page, below photo. Use Border Maker to punch a 12-inch frame chain border. Cut in half and adhere below paper ribbon.
- Use Lovable Mini Pocket Punches to punch hearts from the silver embossed areas of patterned paper. Adhere some of the hearts to the left of journaling. Save a few hearts for the flower centers.
- Layer paper flowers and adhere together. Top with remaining silver hearts.
- Apply flowers to patterned paper square and on upper and lower edge of page. Trim off overhang.

Page 4

- Cut various-sized circles from patterned paper using the Custom Cutting System Circle Patterns.
- Mat each circle with a gray patterned paper circle. Adhere circles in center of green background.
- Apply photo strip to right side using Foam Squares.
- Add title stickers to circles.
- Print or handwrite journaling on White Cardstock. Trim into strips and adhere to page below photos.

Page 3

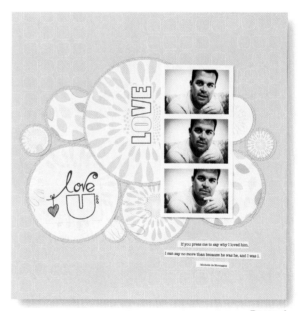

Page 4

HALLOWEEN COUNTDOWN

12 x 12 page for a Magnetic Everyday Display

*My daughter would start wearing her Halloween costume to school in September if I'd let her. I mean, come on, with dress-up **and** candy, Halloween's a pretty big hit with most kids. But we've come up with an adorable, interactive way to help kids keep track of the time. This would make a spooktacular gift for anyone with young children around Halloween time. (Or, if your own kids are getting impatient, make one yourself and give yourself the gift of a little distraction and redirection!)* **Note**: *This project is going to require a trip to the craft store for some tiny magnets.*

Ingredients:

Sleek Black Magnetic Everyday Display

Cheerful Halloween Additions

White Cardstock

Black Sophisticate ABC/123 Stickers

Gratitude Scalloped Tearing Tool

Postage Stamp Place 'n' Punch

12-inch Rotary Trimmer (with Rotary Postage Stamp Blade)

Custom Cutting System (with Circle Patterns)

Magnets (from craft store)

Tape Runner

Foam Squares

Instructions:

• Use a black piece of patterned paper as a base.

• Use the Scalloped Tearing Tool on a piece of dotted patterned paper about 5 inches from the bottom and add to the bottom of the black patterned paper.

• Cut a 12" x 1³/₄" piece of orange patterned paper with the 12-inch Rotary Trimmer and Postage Stamp Blade. Add it across the bottom of the project, as shown.

• Cut a 12" x 1" strip of striped paper and add it across the orange paper.

• Cut a 12" x ¹/₂" strip of black paper using the Rotary Trimmer with the Postage Stamp Blade and add it across the striped paper.

• Cut a green circle using the outside of the small Circle Pattern and green blade and add it to the bottom-right side of the project.

• Add the falling spiders sticker to the upper-left side of the project with Foam Squares.

• Cut two 1¹/₄" x 1¹/₂" pieces of White Cardstock and add them to the green circle.

• Punch 24 postage stamp shapes from various papers and add a magnet to the back of each.

• Add alphabet and title stickers to each, as shown.

• Arrange these on the Everyday Display as shown. They can be rearranged to have the correct countdown number changed each day. Add additional title stickers to the project as shown.

• Add decorative stickers throughout layout.

I LOVE YOU BECAUSE...

Album pages for a 4 x 6 PicFolio® Album

*Mother's Day, Christmas, birthday … There's **never** a bad time to tell Mom you love her. This adorable little 4 x 6 PicFolio® Photo Album goes a step further by showing and telling about all the reasons **why** we love Mom.*

Ingredients:

Reflections 4 x 6 PicFolio® Photo Album

Reflections Storybox Photo Mats

Reflections Decorative ABC Stickers

Reflections Paper Flowers

Reflections Paper Ribbon

Reflections Paper Tags

White Cardstock

White Shimmer Cardstock

Black Dual-Tip Pen

Sweet Heart Maker

12-inch Rotary Trimmer

Foam Squares

Precision Point Adhesive

Tape Runner

Instructions:

Title Page

• Use the Sweet Heart Maker to punch a heart from green paper. Adhere to White Cardstock and trim out. Adhere to blue paper flower with a Foam Square.

• Adhere ABC stickers to blue flower using Foam Squares.

• Trim a piece of paper ribbon to 5½ inches. Adhere to gray tag. Place on gray photo mat and top tag with flower arrangement from above.

• Print or handwrite journaling on White Shimmer Cardstock. Trim and adhere to cover.

Pages

• Using your choice of Storybox photo mats as the backgrounds, adorn each with a strip of paper ribbon, paper flowers or both using Tape Runner and/or Foam Squares.

• Mat photos on various colors of paper. Adhere 1 to each page.

• Print or handwrite journaling on various paper colors and trim into strips. Adhere to each page.

Continued

...you're always up
for a fun outing.

...you always have
yummy treats for us.

...you give hugs
liberally.

...your lap
is always open.

...you came with us to Disneyland.

...you have a great sense of humor.

...you taught me to love animals.

...you never fail to make me feel special.

FATHER'S DAY

Digital layout for an 8 x 8 Photo Panel

OK, you're going to want to brush your teeth after this one because it's so sweet. This is a Digital Photo Panel you can create using Creative Memories StoryBook Creator 4.0 Software. Then you can upload your project to Creative Memories' website and they'll mail the finished Photo Panel right to your door. Put together this adorable little Father's Day gift – in less than an hour – and he'll love it for years. Who else would like this? Everyone!

Ingredients:

StoryBook Creator 4.0 Software

Rugged Digital Power® Palette

Font: Base '02

Instructions:

- Open a blank 8 x 8 Photo Panel project.
- Add Rugged Paper 07 to your background.
- Add a photo and flatten. Cut into a circle. Move the photo so the left side is off the panel.
- Insert Rugged Frame 9. Resize and position in front of the photo as shown.
- Add a white circle. Add Rugged Frame 9 and position it over the top, resizing the titles so the circle fills the frame. Repeat this step. Resize and position the frame and circles as shown on the right side of the layout.
- Insert the "Dad" title and place on top of the top frame and circle combo.
- Insert a text box and type the sentiment using Base '02 as the font. Match the font color to the "Dad" title.

THANKFUL TREE
12 x 12 layout for a Magnetic Everyday Display

Sometimes the "thanks" part of Thanksgiving gets lost somewhere between the decorative napkin holders and the buttery, golden niblets. Here's a way to get the important stuff right up on the wall – and get everyone involved in the process! This is a sensationally simple idea that lets you engage the whole family without overwhelming anyone. You can make this project together before the holidays. Or, try cutting the paper strips in advance and passing them out to everyone to write on during Thanksgiving dinner. Attach them after dinner (while everyone's peacefully snoozing in front of the TV), and you'll have a beautiful gift to leave behind and thank your hosts!

Ingredients:

Chocolate Weathered Magnetic Everyday Display

Gratitude Paper & Photo Mat Pack

Gratitude Title Stickers

Espresso Cardstock

Brown Dual-Tip Pen

Corner Maker

Foam Squares

Tape Runner

Instructions:

• Trim a piece of the blue patterned paper down to 11½" x 11½." Adhere it to the center of a piece of Espresso Cardstock.

• Cut orange circle-patterned paper into 3" x 12" strips. Align these strips along the edge of your Everyday Display.

• Adhere the layout to the center of the orange pattern papers with magnets.

• Cut the brown foil-patterned paper into five ¾" x 12" strips. Trim one to each of the following lengths: 10½," 9," 7," 5" and 3." Adhere the strips as shown to create your tree.

• Print or handwrite, "I AM THANKFUL FOR..." on a tan photo mat. Trim and then outline with a brown pen. Adhere to the tree with Foam Squares as shown.

• Cut orange, tan and green photo mats into ½-inch strips. Trim to various lengths and journal with a brown pen. (You may also want to edge each strip with the pen.) Adhere the strips as desired to finish your tree.

• Cut a triangle by hand from the brown foil-patterned paper. Adhere it to the top of your tree.

• Add any additional journaling strips to the ribbon with clothespins.

• Adhere a title sticker to a tan photo mat. Round the corners of the title box using the Corner Maker and attach it to the ribbon with mini clothespins.

HOLIDAY TRADITIONS

Album pages for a 12 x 12 scrapbook album

We try to keep the focus of the season on giving to others. Some of our favorite causes to support are the local food bank, animal shelters, and the Angel Tree. The kids enjoy picking out items for donation and knowing we helped out others makes our hearts happy!

Holiday traditions aren't necessarily something you give. They're something you keep. But by keeping an ongoing album that celebrates your favorite holiday traditions, you'll be better prepared to share those traditions – and, hopefully, pass them down. And a sense of heritage like that is a gift more precious than gold – for anyone in the family.

Ingredients:

12 x 12 Coverset

12 x 12 White Scrapbook Pages

Holidazzle Paper & Photo Mat Pack

Holidazzle ABC & Title Stickers

Holidazzle Embellishments

Holidazzle Epoxy Stickers

Noel Paper & Photo Mat Pack

Reflections Tone-on-Tone Paper

White Cardstock

White Simple Monogram Stickers

Black Dual-Tip Pen

Pink Dual-Tip Pen

12-inch Rotary Trimmer

Border Maker System (with Scallop Stitch Cartridge)

Custom Cutting System (with Circle Patterns)

Foam Squares

Tape Runner

Instructions:

Page 1

- Trim a piece of striped patterned paper to 8½" x 9¼." Adhere to blue patterned Reflections paper. Adhere two 3" x 4" photos on upper half.
- Use Custom Cutting System Circle Patterns to cut snowflakes from patterned paper. Adhere across bottom of photos using Foam Squares.
- Apply title to bottom edge of striped paper using monogram stickers. Add title stickers above.
- Punch an 8½-inch scallop border from White Cardstock using the Border Maker. Adhere to top of striped paper.
- Print or handwrite journaling on White Cardstock. Trim into strips and adhere as shown.

Page 2

- Cut a 7¼" x 12" rectangle of Holidazzle green polka dot paper. Then cut a 4¼" x 12" rectangle of ornament paper. Adhere to White Cardstock background. Cover the seam between papers with striped-blue paper ribbon.
- Adhere a 5" x 7" photo matted on White Cardstock, on right side of page. Use Foam Squares to adhere a title sticker to left of photo.
- Using a scrap of the green polka dot paper, use the Custom Cutting System Circle Patterns to cut several green circles. Use Foam Squares to adhere the polka dots randomly to the bottom half of the page.
- Print or handwrite journaling on White Cardstock. Trim into strips and adhere as shown.

Believe

Getting to have brunch with Santa is one of the highlights of our Christmas Season! Besides the yummy breakfast buffett at the clubhouse, there is nothing like being able to deliver our wish lists in person to the jolly old elf himself!

December 2009

Page 2

Page 3

- Trim Noel white-patterned paper to 9½" x 9½." Adhere to Holidazzle polka dot paper. Mat photos on blue paper and adhere to page.
- Use pink pen to draw stitching around edge of white patterned paper.
- Trim piece of pink paper to 11" x 1¼." Trim ends and draw stitching with black pen. Adhere to bottom of page. Apply title sticker to center with Foam Square.
- Draw a bowed line with black pen near top of Noel white paper. Apply epoxy stickers. Write journaling using pink pen.

Page 4

- Trim Reflections light-blue patterned paper to 9" x 9." Adhere to snowflake paper. Affix six 2¾" x 3¾" photos, matted on White Cardstock to blue paper.
- Cut a 1" x 12" piece of red paper. Adhere across center of page. Trim another piece of red paper to 2" x 12." Loop ends to middle and adhere to form bow. Trim center as needed. Apply ABC stickers and epoxy stickers to green die cut and use Foam Squares to adhere to center of bow.
- Print or handwrite journaling on White Cardstock. Cut into strips and adhere to page.

Page 3

Page 4

COUNTDOWN TO CHRISTMAS

12 x 12 page for a Magnetic Everyday Display

This. Idea. Rocks! It's an adorable little way to not only help kids manage those days before Christmas but also get everyone into the real spirit of the season. Come up with 25 daily activities that will be fun and meaningful for your family. (We've listed some on the next page, but go ahead and customize them to fit your family's beliefs and traditions.) Start out December 1 with all 25 in the To-Do pocket. By the time you've moved them all to the Done pocket, the big day will be here! Make one for yourself or give it as a gift to a family you love.

Ingredients:

Sleek White Magnetic Everyday Display

Holidazzle Paper & Photo Mat Pack

Holidazzle Embellishments

Holidazzle Epoxy Stickers

White Shimmer Cardstock

Black Simple ABC/123 Stickers

Black Dual-Tip Pen

Paper Edger

Tag Maker

Custom Cutting System (with Oval Patterns)

Foam Squares

Tape Runner

Instructions:

- Use the colored dots paper as the base of your layout.
- Adhere two 4″ x 6″ photos to green photo mats. Adhere to page, centered near the top of the layout.
- Cut a piece of Santa belt paper to $2\frac{1}{2}″$ x 12.″ Use the Paper Edger on one 12″ edge. Fold this edge over so there is a $\frac{3}{8}″$ flap of stripes showing. Adhere to the layout below the photos.
- Trim another piece of Santa belt paper to $3\frac{1}{4}″$ x 12,″ centering on the belt. Using the largest Oval Custom Cutting Pattern, cut 2 semi-circles above the belt $3\frac{1}{4}″$ apart to create the look of pockets.

- Use Tape Runner adhesive on the back two sides, bottom and center of the Santa belt paper. Adhere $1\frac{1}{4}″$ down from the striped flap. Cut a green photo mat to $4\frac{1}{2}″$ x $3\frac{1}{4}.″$ Adhere each inside the pockets as shown.
- Either computer generate or handwrite the titles, "To Do" and "Done" for each pocket. Edge around each title with the black pen.
- Using the ABC stickers, add the title "Christmas Activities." Add the Christmas tree die cut and pink snowflake epoxy sticker, as shown.

Continued

Shovel your neighbor's sidewalk

Bake Gingerbread Cookies

Sing "Jingle Bells" as joyfully as you can.

Make your Christmas Wish List

Have hot chocolate with lots of marshmallows

Countdown to Christmas Tags

Ingredients:

Holidazzle Paper & Photo Mat Pack

White Shimmer Cardstock

Tag Maker

Tape Runner

Instructions:

- Using the Tag Maker, punch 25 tags from various photo mats.
- Journal 25 Christmas activities to do as you count down to Christmas.
- Cut each piece of White Shimmer Cardstock to $1\frac{1}{4}''$ x $2''$ and adhere to the punched tag.
- Slide the tags into the pockets on your Countdown to Christmas page.

Here are 25 ideas:

Take your family holiday photo.

Make a snowman or draw one!

String a popcorn garland for your tree.

Answer the phone saying, "Happy Holidays."

Tell someone you love them.

Mail your holiday cards.

Watch "A Christmas Story."

Hang a wreath on your front door.

Go caroling.

Shovel your neighbor's sidewalk.

Have hot chocolate with lots of marshmallows.

Give back to your community.

Write a letter to Santa.

Bake gingerbread cookies.

Go sledding.

Make a gingerbread house.

Call a long-distance friend or relative.

Make your wish list.

Watch "Miracle on 34th Street."

Bring food to your local food shelf.

Participate in a local give-a-gift program.

Hang your stockings.

Watch "Rudolph the Red-Nosed Reindeer."

Sing "Jingle Bells" as joyfully as you can.

Read "The Night Before Christmas."

HOLIDAY GIFTS

Serving Suggestions

When I was a kid and we would go to my grandparents' for a holiday meal, there was always that moment. We were at the table. The food was on the table. And we would all pause to say grace and be thankful for all the deliciousness we were about to enjoy. And it would all smell so good, I couldn't help peeking.

And when I did, I remember seeing the turkey or the ham or the roast – beautifully perched on Grandma's "company platter." It was big and silver and when you saw it, you knew you were in for something special. Now, I had plenty of wonderful meals with my grandparents. But when that platter came out it meant Grandma had put a little extra heart into this one.

When you follow one of the recipes in this book, you'll be creating something unique and special for someone you love. And if you ask me, it deserves the platter.

TRY SOME OF THESE FUN SERVING SUGGESTIONS

Let me give you an example of what I mean when I call these "serving suggestions." For our very first Valentine's Day together, my thoughtful husband Keith (who, it must be said, is a very fast learner) made me a scrapbook.

When I entered the door from work, I first saw a bouquet of flowers and a note, which led me on a scavenger hunt throughout the house. It was incredibly cute and, when I finally found the scrapbook – which held his thoughts on everything we'd lived through since the day we met in that fateful airport security line – I appreciated it even more!

Leave it behind

If the gift you're giving is to a hostess or parent (someone you are visiting), then find a great spot to leave the gift behind. Maybe with a bottle of wine or a treat, and a note inviting them to "sit back and enjoy." I promise, you will soon get a joy-filled call, thanking you for the gift!

Tuck it in the suitcase as a souvenir

If the gift you're giving is to a special guest, find a subtle way to sneak it into a suitcase or carry-on bag. They'll find it when they get home and you'll get that same joy-filled call!

Give it as a group

For some of those milestone events, it's fun to present these gifts as a group. (Especially if you got some help from others in creating this gift.) Everyone can share what they contributed, and looking through the gift will be a huge part of the get together. Everyone loves to "remember when."

The traveling box

I heard this great story about a mom who started a new tradition in her family. In addition to all the gifts she gave at the holidays, she hand-made an extra gift and put it in a traveling box. Now, whoever receives the gift in that box this year makes a home-made gift to give to someone else in the family next year. What a great idea!

Tie it up

Tie a big, luxurious, satin ribbon around the album or gift. They will know what's inside is a **big** deal.

Bring it out for dessert after dinner

Once everyone's happily fed and comfortably full, bring out your really sweet gift to top it all off. It will give everyone an excuse to sit around the table together and laugh as they thumb through the album.

Better than a gift card

Oh, the gift card. They've become so popular as gifts because they're easy, practical and flexible. But they seem so ... impersonal, don't they? If you make a personalized photo gift, maybe just tuck a gift card inside. The sleeves of a PicFolio® Album would be great for this. Or clip your gift onto a Magnetic Everyday Display with the mini clothespins!

SKETCHES

Many of our projects in this book include just enough specifics to get you started – particularly when you're working on a full-size album. Sketches can be a great source of continuing inspiration. Let these give you ideas for finishing your album or beginning a whole new project! Wherever you see little circles, those are stickers. Lines? Those are your journaling spaces. Photos? Well, by now you know what photos are. The rest of the shapes indicate paper. Have fun!

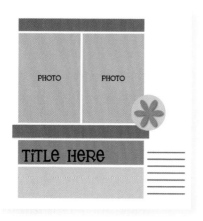

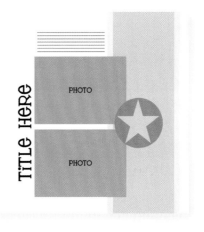

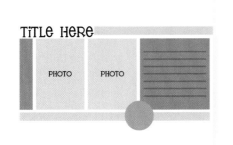

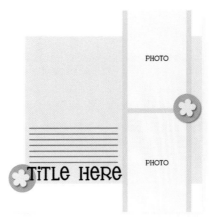

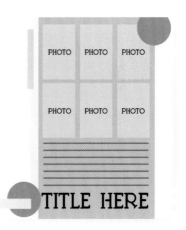

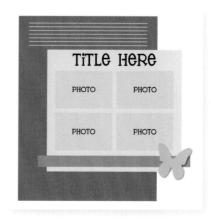

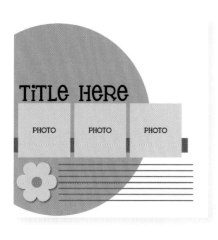

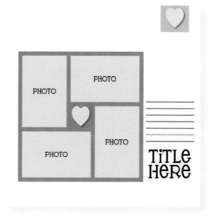

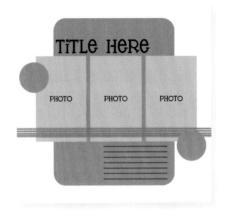

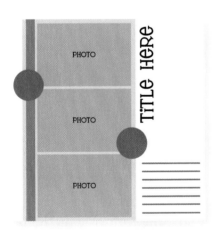

SUGGESTIONS

GLOSSARY

Curious what we mean when we say "4 x 6 PicFolio® Photo Album?"
We thought you might be, so these are descriptions of the foundational
products used in this book. As always, if you are unsure where to begin,
please reach out to any Creative Memories Consultant.
You can find one at creativememories.com (.ca).

12 x 12 Coversets and Scrapbook Pages

A Creative Memories coverset and pages combine to create possibly the most durable and best-made album in the world. Each album is perfect for projects that need a little space, or room to grow – like family heritage albums or holiday traditions albums – since they expand to hold up to 40 pages with their patented Flex-Hinge® Binding.

8 x 8 Coversets and Scrapbook Pages

An 8 x 8 album is a wonderful, easy-to-complete gift size for special events like weddings, new babies or a special trip. They also work perfectly for "slice of life" projects. For example, in this book, we used this album for the Things We Love project.

11 x 14 PicFolio Photo Album

The 11 x 14 PicFolio Album makes it look like you did a ton of work, but really, it couldn't be any easier. All you do is drop the photos and decorative cards into the pocket pages. Your gift looks amazing, and only you know how easy it was!

4 x 6 PicFolio Photo Album

This little album is perfect for small projects or for when you want something portable. One of the things that make it special is the cover strap that secures the album closed. It also wraps around in the back to create an instant easel. Give this little album to someone as a gift. It's perfect to put on a desk, put on a table or take along wherever you go!

Pages and Protectors

Pages are the heart of an album. We love the versatility of the traditional scrapbook album page . . . anything goes! (Just be sure to top it off with a page protector to keep them safe.) And we adore the simplicity a pocket page offers. A side loading sleeve lets you easily use full 12 x 12 digital prints in your album. So whatever your project needs, we have the page for it. Questions about pages? Any Creative Memories Consultant will be happy to answer them!

SUGGESTIONS

Magnetic Everyday Displays

We love these! Why? Because they are so quick to put together, but look so impressive! And the magnets let you display whatever you'd like today, then switch it up and display something different tomorrow. They make amazing gifts, whether you're making a special statement (like "I love you"), welcoming a new baby or just sharing the little things in life that make you feel happy.

8 x 8 Recipe Quick Album

The 8 x 8 Recipe Quick Album is designed to help you make a treasure of your family's favorite recipes. Whether they're Grandma's peanut butter cookies or Aunt Marie's enchiladas, they'll seem even more special in this album. It's also a perfect way to share things like your best wishes for a newlywed couple with your recipes for a happy life together.

Digital Products

In this book we've featured a variety of digital projects: Wall Print posters, Photo Panels, Page Prints and more. A great thing about digital products is that you create them once, then print as many as you want! For all of the digital projects featured in this book, we used Creative Memories' StoryBook Creator 4.0 Software. Whatever you choose to create, just follow the instructions in the software to upload and order your project from digital.creativememories.com and it will show up in your mailbox!

SUGGESTIONS

You've got your ideas, now get started! Use this guide to plan a list of the projects you'd like to create . . . for yourself or for someone else.

Recipient: _____ Occasion/Date: _____

Project: _____

Supplies and photos needed: _____

_____

_____

_____

_____

_____

_____

Recipient: _____ Occasion/Date: _____

Project: _____

Supplies and photos needed: _____

_____

_____

_____

_____

_____

_____

Recipient: _____ Occasion/Date: _____

Project: _____

Supplies and photos needed: _____

_____

_____

_____

_____

_____

_____

Recipient: _____ Occasion/Date: _____

Project: _____

Supplies and photos needed: _____

_____

_____

_____

_____

_____

_____

SUGGESTIONS

Recipient: _____ Occasion/Date: _____

Project: _____

Supplies and photos needed:_____

_____

_____

_____

_____

_____

_____

Recipient: _____ Occasion/Date: _____

Project: _____

Supplies and photos needed:_____

_____

_____

_____

_____

_____

_____

Recipient: _____ Occasion/Date: _____

Project: _____

Supplies and photos needed: _____

_____

_____

_____

_____

_____

_____

Recipient: _____ Occasion/Date: _____

Project: _____

Supplies and photos needed: _____

_____

_____

_____

_____

_____

_____

SUGGESTIONS

Nancy O'Dell is an Emmy Award-winning entertainment journalist, who has proven to be a force as a host, author, producer and entrepreneur. She's currently co-host of the most watched entertainment news program in the world, *Entertainment Tonight*. Previously, she anchored *Access Hollywood* for 13 years and has contributed to CBS's *The Early Show* as well as NBC's *Today* show and *Dateline*. As co-host of Oprah Winfrey's premiere primetime show, *Your Own Show*, on the OWN Network, Nancy fulfilled a career dream of working with Oprah. With 20 years of live television experience, Nancy has hosted countless network specials, including multiple *Emmy Awards Red Carpet* shows, as well as *The Live Golden Globes Arrivals Special* and *The Tournament of Roses Parade*. She also rang in 2011 on Fox's *New Year's Eve Live*. Nancy's previous books include "FULL OF LIFE: Mom-to-Mom Tips I Wish Someone Told Me When I Was Pregnant," and "FULL OF LOVE: Mom-to-Mom Advice for Enriching Families With Simple Photo Albums and Scrapbooking." As a designer, Nancy has her own line of outdoor furniture called "Red Carpet by Nancy O'Dell" and a growing line of scrapbooking products with Creative Memories. She is a self-described "scrapbooking fiend" who scraps "anything and everything." Nancy is a National Vice President of the Muscular Dystrophy Association, the ALS National Ambassador and a co-host of the annual MDA Telethon. Nancy has been working with MDA ever since her mother was diagnosed with ALS in 2008. In August 2009, MDA, Nancy and Nancy's family formed a foundation in her mother's memory called Betty's Battle: Fighting ALS. Nancy also serves as an International Board Member of Best Buddies, a nonprofit organization dedicated to establishing a global volunteer movement that creates opportunities for one-to-one friendships and employment for people with intellectual and developmental disabilities. Nancy lives in Los Angeles with her husband, her two stepsons and her daughter.